WORDS OF LIFE

EASTER EDITION

JANUARY–APRIL 1995

**Donated by
Major Ellen Tackaberry**

HODDER AND STOUGHTON
and
THE SALVATION ARMY

ISBN 0 340 61251 7

Typeset by Hewer Text Composition Services, Edinburgh.

Printed and bound in Great Britain by
Cox & Wyman, Reading, Berks.

Hodder and Stoughton Ltd
A Division of Hodder Headline PLC
338 Euston Road
London NW1 3BH

All unattributed verse is by the author
Commissioner Harry Read

CONTENTS

'Faith Works'

Sundays

Words of Adoration
Words of Grace
Words of Reinforcement
Words of Insight
Words of Praise
Words of Prayer

ABBREVIATIONS USED FOR BIBLE VERSIONS

AV   Authorised (King James) Version
GNB   Good News Bible
JB   Jerusalem Bible
JBP   J B Phillips – The New Testament in Modern English, 1972 edition
JM   James Moffatt Bible
LB   Living Bible – Kenneth Taylor
NASB   New American Standard Bible
NEB   New English Bible
NIV   New International Version
NKJV   New King James Version
RAV   Revised Authorised Version
REB   Revised English Bible
RSV   Revised Standard Version

Because of the world-wide popularity of the NIV, *Words of Life* uses it constantly. However, other versions also have great merit and, but for their more limited use, could also have functioned as our basic version. We therefore suggest that you continue to use the translation which appeals to you most, occasionally turning to another version for additional insights. Where *Words of Life* uses a passage of Scripture more than once, reading aloud, or the use of another version to give variety, is strongly recommended.

OTHER ABBREVIATIONS:

SASB   The Song Book of The Salvation Army, 1986
H&H   Happiness and Harmony – a supplementary song and chorus book, (Salvationist Publishing and Supplies, Ltd.)
WoL   Words of Life

'*Words of Life*' has been transcribed into Braille by Roy Tysoe and is available from: RNIB, PO Box 173, Peterborough, PE22 OWS, England. Telephone No. 0345 023153.

WORDS OF ADORATION

READING 1 TIMOTHY 6:11–16
'Fight the good fight of the faith. Take hold of the eternal life to which you were called' (v.12a, NIV).

GOD CONTINUES to be with us as we move into this new year. Whatever we need of grace and wisdom is already assured (*2 Cor 12:9; James 1:5*). We can cope! Our key verse reminds us that the fight of faith is a continuing warfare, we therefore face this new year in a spirit of challenge. There are battles to be won, spiritual gains to be made, lessons to be learned, all to make us more able to fulfil our calling and shape us into the likeness of Jesus (*Rom 8:29 NEB*).

The two verbs pursue (*v.11*) and fight (*v.12*) are strong verbs reflecting the importance of the virtues God wishes us to develop, and the factual conflict between good and evil. They are splendid New Year's Day verbs because we want this new year to be even better than the old. No good reason exists why this should not happen. Like Timothy we need reminding of the sovereignty of God, and his majesty (*v.15*). With a God like that, we who serve him have overwhelming resources to enable us to succeed.

PRAYER:
Let me but live this year, Lord, in your sight,
My heart and mind in harmony with yours,
Aware of you, your glory and your might,
Your willingness to share your gracious powers.
Set firm my mind all good things to pursue,
And when joys come, or even sorrow's load,
All will be well, if I but walk with you,
My hand in yours along my chosen road.

For you are God. In majesty you reign,
Your mighty hands this universe enfold;
And yet you bid me Christlikeness attain;
My aspirations prompt to be more bold!

You are my God! Your love this year has made;
With hope I face the future, unafraid.

PRAYER SUBJECT: Those who are overwhelmed with despair.

THE DESPERATION OF FEAR

READING NUMBERS 22:1–6

'Now Balak son of Zippor saw all that Israel had done to the Amorites, and Moab was terrified because there were so many people. Indeed, Moab was filled with dread because of the Israelites' (vv.2, 3, NIV).

WE CAN UNDERSTAND Balak's fear and concern when he realised that the Israelite host was approaching his frontier. He would know the fate which befell the Amorites and fear that a similar fate awaited him and his people. It was the ancient belief that curses as well as blessings, once launched, continued to do their work; not unreasonably, therefore, Balak considered his options and chose to approach the proven seer, Balaam, for assistance.

21:23–35
v.4
Gen 27:30–38

v.5

Not too many twentieth-century insights should be read into this event but one wonders how different the history of the world might have been had kings and people followed the way of co-operation instead of conflict. Earlier, Moses had attempted a peaceful route into the Promised Land but King Sihon chose to fight. Must not God, who is the Father of all people, have preferred the way of peace to the way of slaughter? In support of this, we recall the Mosaic Law requirement that aliens should be well treated, even loved. Warfare with all its cruelty, consequences and difficult questions was not inevitable.

21:21, 22

Exod 22:21
Lev 19:34

Hindsight tells us that Balak had a better option than Balaam. His fear could have made him more aware of Israel's God who would have treated him most mercifully. How greatly we need to cultivate sensitivity towards our heavenly Father.

TO PONDER

If only we were sensitive enough
To be aware of God and read the signs,
Would not our choices smooth the places rough
As we co-operate with God's designs?

THE SEER AT WORK

READING NUMBERS 22:7–14
'God said to Balaam, "Do not go with them. You must not put a curse on those people, because they are blessed"' (v.12, NIV).

BEARING the fee for divination the elders of Moab and Midian approached Balaam. In the marvellous pace with which this fascinating story is told we do not know whether Balaam was totally pagan or, in some undisclosed way, had a special relationship with Israel's God. Did he have a check-list of gods which he used according to the nationality and needs of his patrons, in this instance making appropriate reference to Jehovah? The seer emerges from these verses in a good light but other passages of Scripture treat him much more severely. Suffice it to say that after settling his visitors down for the night, Balaam commenced his work.

We marvel at the willingness of God to respond to people regardless of their spiritual condition. The interview with God was rapidly concluded, Balaam being left in no doubt that those whom God had blessed were not to be cursed. To Balaam's credit he communicated this message in the most positive manner to the princes of Moab and Midian.

God's readiness to communicate with those who, in one sense or another, are opposed to him is astounding and rewarding. He took the initiative on the Damascus Road changing Saul, the resolute enemy, into Paul, the resourceful servant. We also recall, with relief and gratitude, that God came to us in our confusion and distress, making us aware, not only of his authority, but also of his tenderness and acceptance. We merited only judgment but received grace upon grace.

v.7

31:8–16; Deut 23:4–5; 2 Pet 2:15; Jude 11; Rev 2:14
v.8

v.9

v.12

v.13

Acts 9:1–19

God presses through the barriers to speak
The words of grace which only he can say.
Does he not come as we his mercy seek
Impelled by needs demanding that we pray?

PRAISE

HIS FINEST HOUR

READING NUMBERS 22:15–20
'But Balaam answered them, "Even if Balak gave me his palace filled with silver and gold, I could not do anything great or small to go beyond the command of the Lord my God"' (v.18, NIV).

v.15

v.12

BALAK, King of Moab, refused to be denied. When his princes returned with Balaam's negative response he sent additional and more influential princes to win Balaam's co-operation. Fear is nothing if not persistent. No doubt also, Balak reasoned that his riches would be of little value to him in the event of defeat at the hands of the Israelites, therefore, he would be wise to invest them in a possible victory. But Balaam remained steadfast. The word that God had given him was a word by which he would stand.

As we read this encounter between the rich king and the soothsayer we can only be impressed. No aspiring saint can hope to make a better statement of loyalty and obedience. Facing the Emperor Charles V, who was to brand him a heretic, Martin Luther's words 'Here I stand – I can do no other' although much braver and, historically, much more significant, were no better minted than those of Balaam.

v.19

Unfortunately, Balaam's words were stronger than his resolve, a fact which probably accounted for his return to God in search of further guidance. Was he seeking a less arduous path?

AN
AFFIRMATION

I have to be obedient to the Lord,
Fulfil his blessed will, obey his word,
I could not, if I would, usurp his power,
Deny his right to rule each single hour.

The Lord our God alone is King, and reigns
Alone, unaided, he all things sustains,
None but a fool would try to stay his hand
Or thwart the mighty blessings he has planned.

BLINDNESS

READING NUMBERS 22:21–31
'Balaam got up in the morning, saddled his donkey and went with the princes of Moab' (v.21, NIV).

BALAAM'S PERSISTENCE prevailed and God disclosed another plan. Perhaps the prophet rose eagerly the next day to set out for his meeting with Balak. Perhaps he rose a little too eagerly for God! There seems to be some conflict between verses 20 and 22. In the former we read that God gave permission, in the latter that God was angry with Balaam for going. Walter Riggins suggests that there are legitimate grounds for changing 'when he went' to 'as he went'. This allows us to assume that God knew Balaam regarded the exercise as one which would yield him riches and prestige. Kenneth Taylor follows this perception with, 'God was angry about Balaam's eager attitude'. Far from maintaining his high-minded stance of loyalty and obedience, some form of compromise of benefit to himself was being contemplated.

v.20

v.22(LB)
v.18(WoL 4
Jan)

Greed and self-will are but two of the sins which cause spiritual blindness. Blinkered by faults, people today are as unseeing of God as Balaam was then. The divine humour seems to shine out through the gift of speech to the ass. As though God was saying:

v.23

v.28

> *A common ass displays more sense,*
> *Is more perceptive of my ways*
> *Than prophets shrouded by pretence,*
> *Beguiled by wealth and princely praise.*

Having beaten the ass mercilessly and received the ass's rebuke, Balaam's eyes were opened and he became aware of the angel of the Lord barring his way. It was in this moment Balaam realised he was perfectly free to disobey the word of God, but that he could not do so with impunity. God has always required obedience from his followers.

v.31

THE CHALLENGER

READING NUMBERS 22:32–35
'I have come here to oppose you because your path is a reckless one before me' (v.32b, NIV).

v.23.

THE STORY of Balaam illustrates the fact that it is possible to be on the right road but in the wrong spirit, the story also illustrates the constraining nature of divine judgment. When the donkey, far more perceptive than the prophet, saw the angel standing in the roadway with drawn sword, he turned into the nearby open field. Balaam, failing to see the reason for this, beat the animal and forced it back into the road but this time, with considerably less room to manoeuvre, his foot was crushed against the wall. Rather surprisingly, this man, who was prepared to see signs where others saw none, again failing to evaluate the incident, beat the donkey and drove it forward, whereupon, at a place where there was no room to turn, the creature lay down when faced by the angel only to be beaten again. It was at this point the donkey was given the power of speech.

v.25.

v.27.

v.28.

vv. 12,20

Obviously, it would have been better had Balaam accepted God's first instruction and not sought an amended decision, but we conclude that Balaam was allowed to proceed because he had lessons to learn, as had Balak and we ourselves.

Does not God challenge us when we walk the wrong road, or even the right road but in the wrong spirit? Increasingly, we find ourselves constrained, with diminishing space for manoeuvring, until we face the truth that his justice bars the way. However, and oh! so happily, we find that with his justice there is mercy. He wills, not our destruction but salvation.

A PRAYER

O Lord, you are most merciful,
Most tender and most bountiful,
Your love has reached me, even me,
And set my sin-bound spirit free.

THE PAGAN MIND

READING NUMBERS 22:36–41
'Balak said to Balaam, "Did I not send you an urgent summons? Why didn't you come to me? Am I really not able to reward you?" (v.37, NIV).

BALAK WAS ACCUSTOMED to idolatry, to worshipping mute gods which had no opinion to express. His brand of Baal worship had an emphasis on fertility, giving rise to a dominant, and, to its worshippers, a not undesirable requirement of engaging in fertility rites. Probably because Baalism lacked morality Balak assumed that spiritual powers could be manipulated. He had but to find the right practitioner, pay the right price, and all would be well. Hence his approach to Balaam.

cf.25:1–3

vv.4b–7

Balak saw no need to change himself. Threatened, as he rightly observed, by the people who had 'come out of Egypt', (such a description seems to imply knowledge of Israel's pilgrimage and the power of Israel's God), Balak still thought of confrontation rather than accommodation. If Israel had been blessed, then, in all probability, that blessing could be neutralised by a curse.

v.5b

v.6

We acknowledge the fact that those who stood in Israel's way to Canaan represented a primitive form of religion. Even so, though Balak was a product of his times, paganism bears similar marks in every culture. Significantly, it looks for solutions without moral and spiritual connotations, including a readiness to employ the 'powers of this dark world' to achieve its ends. If only pagans would turn to the God who is so near.

Eph 6:12

Why do we struggle with our daily load,
Bowed down by our responsibilities,
Our choices which become anxieties,
The problems which beset our winding road
When all the time our Father God is near
To share the burden, banish all our fear?

TO PONDER

WORDS OF GRACE

READING 1 PETER 1:1, 2

'To God's elect . . . who have been chosen . . .' (vv.1a, 2a,NIV).

THE CHRISTIANS to whom Peter was writing lived in a large area as verse 1 indicates. Peter uses the word 'dispersion' (RSV, RAV, cf REB), a word which referred specifically to Jews who were scattered abroad (Jer 25: 34, RSV; John 7:35, REB; Acts 2:5–11), applying it to them. While there would be church members who were 'Jews of the dispersion' many more would be converts from paganism (v.14; 2:9,10). The purpose of this letter was to strengthen the flock as they faced various trials (vv.6, 7).

It would not escape the attention of his readers, that Peter (the name means rock) was the name given by Jesus to Simon. '. . . you are Peter, and on this rock I will build my church, and the gates of Hades will not overcome it' (Matt 16:18). By association, they would be aware of the indestructibility of the Church of Christ.

Peter sought to strengthen the people by further applying other Jewish words to them. They were the elect, the chosen. They may well have come from the excesses of paganism, slavery or city slums, but they were still the chosen of God.

> *If God thinks well of me*
> *What matters if the world thinks otherwise?*
> *If God has chosen me*
> *From his strong grasp no hand my soul can prise.*

Their special place in the heart and strategy of God afforded them a strength and stability without parallel. 'If God is for us, who can be against us? (Rom 8:31). God's chosen have all the resources of heaven available to them.

PRAYER
> *In shame, Lord, I confess, I chose not thee,*
> *But in thy mercy thou hast chosen me,*
> *In chosenness I find my liberty,*
> *My hope, fulfilment and security.*

PRAYER
SUBJECT
> *Christians suffering persecution.*

A GREAT ADVENTURE

READING NUMBERS 23:1–5
'And Balaam said unto Balak, "Stand by thy burnt offering. and I will go: peradventure the Lord will come to meet me . . ." And he went to an high place' (v.3, AV).

SEVEN altars, seven bulls, seven rams, Balaam, the sorcerer, was playing the perfect figure of seven as hard as he possibly could: he knew this was a hard assignment. With the offering made, not to a pagan god but to Jehovah, Balaam proceeded to a high place hoping that God would meet with him.

v.1

Modern translations use the word 'perhaps' in place of the AV's 'peradventure.' The words are interchangeable, but recent versions lose the element of hazard, of adventure, in the exercise. Balaam was not short of courage. To walk up to a barren mountain top, hoping to meet with a God who had denied him the right to go to Balak, who later modified his plan and gave permission and had then been most angry with him, required a great deal of courage. Undoubtedly, Balaam was embarked on a great adventure. He was deliberately crossing the threshold from the known to the unknown. We pause to reaffirm that we who are the people of God can also find the stimulating challenge of adventure and discovery as we seek to know God and his will for us. But, unlike Balaam, we know God as Father.

22:12, 22:20
22:22–33

> *To meet you, Lord, I step into the unknown,*
> *I leave this realm of sights and sounds and things*
> *To meet you in that world which is your own,*
> *That world of deep, mysterious happenings.*
> *Adventure, Lord, is found within your will;*
> *You make me partner in a great emprise,*
> *Give strength for battle, furnish me with skill,*
> *And in the life of faith, you make me wise.*
>
> *Grant me, O Lord, a vision of your power,*
> *That I might boldly serve you every hour.*

PRAISE

BALAAM'S FIRST PROPHECY

READING NUMBERS 23:5–12
'Who can count the dust of Jacob or number the fourth part of Israel?'
(v.10a, NIV).

Gen 12:2;
28:14

IN HIS ENCOUNTER with God on the mountain top Balaam discovered that God was faithful to the promises he had made to Abraham and the Patriarchs. Beginning with Abraham and Sarah's only son, Isaac, through Jacob and his sons, Israel actually became a great nation.

v.9b

We wonder whether God shared with Balaam other promises he had made to Israel concerning their destiny and the blessedness he intended for them. Certainly, something has to account for Balaam's comment on Israel's separateness as a nation, that could not have been deduced: also to make him say, 'Let me die the death of the righteous, and may my end be like theirs'!

v.10b

v.5
22:31

But if Balaam had reflected upon his adventure he would have deduced that Israel's God was not only a living God but that he was approachable. After meeting the angel bearing a sword on the highway, the prophet would have been justifiably fearful at the prospect of meeting God, but the God he met showed concern for his people and was more interested in blessing than cursing. The impact on this pagan prophet, a master of sorcery, possibly also spiritism and the black arts, must have been enormous.

v.8

cf v.23

v.1

Had Balaam thought further he would have realised that this God had no need to be placated by offering seven bulls and seven rams on seven altars. His will was paramount and being a God determined to plant his chosen people in a chosen land, acceptance and obedience counted far more than offerings.

PRAISE

The God of Israel is alive;
He meets with those who seek him still,
And shows he keeps his promises
To all who seek to keep his will.

THE HEART OF THE MATTER

READING NUMBERS 23:6–12
'How can I curse those whom God has not cursed? How can I denounce those whom the Lord has not denounced?' (v.8, NIV).

IF ANY DOUBTS concerning the genuineness of Balaam have been entertained because at one stage a donkey was given human speech, or if he has been devalued because it took a talking animal to bring him to his senses, this oracle, surely, redresses the balance. It is a prophecy worthy of a man who has just had an authentic interview with God.

22:28

We take careful note of our key verse. When the two questions were asked, one answer alone was possible, thereby strengthening Balaam and weakening Balak at the same time. However, implicit in these rhetorical questions given by God to Balaam, questions which enabled him to handle his situation effectively, lies a truth relevant for all time, namely, that people are required to accept God's values. Rephrasing Balaam's question makes the point even clearer, 'How can I support that which God does not support?'

vv.11,12

Every society today faces moral and social problems of crucial importance. Although there are many grey areas where uncertainty confuses the process of decision-making, and Christians might well find themselves out of step with each other, more influence would be exerted if we concluded that we could not support that which God does not support. And in that realm of personal religion where attitudes are formed helping to determine the kind of people we are, and the quality of the witness we make, the questions God used to resolve Balaam's thinking are even more important.

> *Lord, let me live so close to you*
> *That much more I might understand*
> *Your heart and mind, your point of view,*
> *And be and do as you have planned.*

A PRAYER

BALAAM'S SECOND ORACLE

READING NUMBERS 23:13–26
'God is not a man, that he should lie, nor a son of man, that he should change his mind. Does he speak and then not act? Does he promise and not fulfil?' (v.19, NIV).

WHATEVER impression we may have of Balaam, God still used him at a critical time in the history of Israel to say some important things about himself and his people. Balaam's refusal to curse Israel reveals his acceptance of God's words, but Balak refused to be impressed, even insisting on another attempt, complete with sacrifices, to change God's mind.

v.25

vv.27–30

Like the first oracle, the second is beautifully expressed. In it the integrity of God is reaffirmed. God does not lie, neither, like a man, does he change his mind. Actions follow his words and he always fulfils his promises.

v.19.

vv.21ff

The latter part of the oracle reveals God's thoughts about Israel. God seems to be looking beyond the obvious flaws to an idealised Israel in whom there is no iniquity or mischief, he confirms his sovereign presence with them; because of it they could celebrate, hence the 'shout of the King is among them'. Israel was immune to sorcery and divination and was to be evidence of the greatness of God's acts, not least their deliverance from Egypt and their certainty of victory in battle. Notwithstanding these divine revelations within the prophecy of Balaam, Balak remained unconvinced. He continued to think of God in human terms persisting with his desire to curse Israel, and depicts the failure of the wilful, insensitive heart to recognise God.

v.21 (REB)

v.21b

vv.22–24

PRAYER

O for a humbler walk with God!
Lord, bend this stubborn heart of mine;
Subdue each rising, rebel thought,
And all my will conform to thine.

(Edward Harland, SASB 445)

DESPERATION

READING NUMBERS 23:27–24:1
'Now when Balaam saw that it pleased the Lord to bless Israel, he did not resort to sorcery as at other times, but turned his face towards the desert' (24:1, NIV).

POOR BEWILDERED BALAK! Following the second oracle when Balaam, instead of pronouncing a curse upon Israel had further blessed them, Balak, somewhat pragmatically yet pathetically, proposed that if Balaam could not curse them, he would settle for him not blessing them! However, after a period of reflection, 23:25
he regained his optimism and suggested that from another vantage point, the 'top of Peor', Balaam might 23:28
secure God's permission to curse the Israelites. The chosen location is interesting because it was the mountain linked with the worship of the local Baal. Perhaps 25:3
Balak hoped the influence of the place would encourage Balaam to prophesy against Israel, but God used it as an occasion to further assert his own authority. Is he not the Lord of all creation?

Again the sacrificial procedure of seven altars with seven bulls and seven rams was followed but Balaam did not even seek a lonely place to meet with God, neither did he engage in sorcery, he simply looked out over the desert where the Israelites were encamped and the inspiration for his third oracle began to flow. 24:1

The king had cause to be desperate. Had he not set himself against the Almighty God? Accustomed to worshipping man-made or imaginary gods which, by definition, had no minds of their own, he was now in conflict with the living God and appeared to be trying to influence, or counsel him. cf Isa 40:13,14

The truth of God is sure and will not change, TO PONDER
Nor yield, as man seeks to manipulate.
It would be odd indeed: completely strange,
If fallen man, the Lord could educate.

THE THIRD ORACLE

READING NUMBERS 24:1–9
'When Balaam looked out and saw Israel encamped tribe by tribe, the Spirit of God came upon him and he uttered his oracle' (v.2,3a, NIV).

Num 2:1–34

THE DESERT must have looked magnificent to Balaam as he gazed out from the top of Peor. Before him stretched the people of God like an immense, living tapestry. In the centre was the Tabernacle, surrounded closely by the Levites on three sides and the Priests on the fourth, who, in turn, were surrounded by the remaining tribes, each tribe camped in a square formation. It was a formidable array. Enough to make any king fear for his future, and for any prophet to be assured that Israel was for blessing not cursing.

v.4

vv.5,6
v.5

vv.7,8, v.9b.

Apparently Balaam went into a trance, falling wide-eyed and prostrate on the ground. Odd though the situation may be to our eyes, Balaam's description of the Hebrew encampment is quite beautiful, sufficiently beautiful for the Jews to take his words and preface every morning service in their synagogues since. Balaam prophesied prosperity, greatness and victory for the nation, and then blessed them.

Ezra 1:1–4
John 19:8–11

There are times when God uses unlikely people to achieve his ends. On this occasion he took a fearful Balak with his determined will to survive, and a pagan soothsayer or sorcerer, to bring glory to his own name. Later, God was to use another pagan king, Cyrus of Persia, conqueror of Babylon. Later still, he used Pontius Pilate. And has he not used very ordinary people, perhaps more frequently, very, very ordinary people, to fulfil his great purposes?

PRAISE

God even speaks through us!
He takes the commonest of tools
To shape his plan divine.
Thank God! He has a place for fools!

WORDS OF REINFORCEMENT

READING 1 PETER 1:1–9
'Grace and peace be yours in abundance' (v.2b, NIV).

AS WE HAVE already noted (*WoL* 8 Jan), the Christians in Asia Minor were living under the threat of a persecution which promised to become even more severe (vv.6,7,). Whether Peter had the evil Nero in mind and the persecution he was to initiate is uncertain, but he was confident that worse was to come. It was out of his care for the flock (John 21:16) that Peter wrote to encourage and build them up in the faith.

In their most difficult situation Peter wished for them grace and peace. Grace is, of course, that free and unconditional favour of God which ever flows towards his children.

Thy sovereign grace to all extends,
Immense and unconfined;
From age to age it never ends;
It reaches all mankind.

(Charles Wesley, SASB 55)

That grace provides all we need for victorious living. As Paul testified, sharing the word God gave him, 'My grace is sufficient for you, for my power is made perfect in weakness' (2 Cor 12:9), we lack for nothing when we have God's grace. Generations of Christians have been grateful for that insight.

Peter also wished peace upon the vulnerable flock. Peace is one of the promises Jesus made to his disciples (John 14:27). It is a promise to us all and is a consequence of his grace. Matthew Henry rightly affirms that 'peace without grace is mere stupidity', but the peace of God guards our hearts and minds in Christ Jesus (Phil 4:7). It is the only peace worth having.

PRAYER
Lord,
Grant me your grace
And let my faith burn bright;
Grant me your peace,
Though troubled be my night.

PRAYER SUBJECT
Regimes which persecute Christians.

THE FOURTH ORACLE

READING NUMBERS 24:10–19
'A star will come out of Jacob; a sceptre will rise out of Israel' (v.17b, NIV).

v.11

vv.11,12

v.14

v.17

ANGERED and exasperated by Balaam, Balak ordered his unhelpful prophet back to his own land. Presumably, Balaam had anticipated this and was ready to affirm that from the beginning he had insisted that he could only speak the words God gave him. For good measure, Balaam launched into an oracle of even greater significance than the others. Those tempted to relegate Balaam to a children's story book because of the talking donkey episode, must surely have to restore him to favour because of the quality of this fourth oracle. If only because of a prophecy many people through the centuries have assumed to be a reference to the Messiah.

Imagine the situation: the People of God, having been in the desert for forty years, were now standing on the threshold of the promised land. Their progress was barred by the Moabites and Midianites under King Balak. We sense their excitement, their desire to occupy the land which by promise was theirs. But, unknown to them, their enemy was coercing a pagan prophet, a proven seer and sorcerer, to put a curse on Israel in order to weaken them in preparation for defeat. However, Israel's God would not be denied and the prophet who was to curse could only bless. Even more, Balaam actually predicted the coming of Israel's Messiah. It was an incredible scenario!

King Balak would know, beyond all doubt, that in opposing Israel, he was opposing Almighty God, and his defeat was sure.

PRAISE

> *Hail Abraham's God and mine!*
> *I join the heavenly lays;*
> *All might and majesty are thine,*
> *And endless praise.*
>
> (Thomas Olivers, SASB 223)

READING NUMBERS 24:12–25
'Even if Balak gave me his palace filled with silver and gold, I could not do anything of my own accord, good or bad, to go beyond the command of the Lord' (v.13a, NIV).

FROM HIS ENCOUNTER with Balak, Balaam emerges as a man of discernment and good judgment. His failure to perceive the presence of the angel was his one demerit. A less honourable prophet could have pronounced worthless curses on Israel and returned home a rich man, confident that since Balak was doomed, he would be immune from any form of retribution. *22:22–34*

However, Balaam chose to obey God. Declarations of obedience, such as his, would grace the biography of any saint. His question, 'How can I curse those whom God has not cursed?' glows with insight and integrity. Whatever followed after, at this stage, Balaam seemed to be well motivated. His prophecies identified the nature of Israel in its phenomenal growth and separation from other nations; its special relationship with God, the divine patronage, the promise of greatness and the promise of victory. Balaam also identified God as unchanging and faithful, a constant support and Israel's guarantor of victory and a bright future. *22:13,18,34b, 38, etc 23:8 23:9,10 23: 20,21 23:22,23a;24:6 23:23b; 24:7b,17 23:24;24:8,9,17b–24*

Unfortunately, Balaam appeared to live below the standard of his insights and his brave uncompromising declarations. No reason is given for his failure to return home, but he is named among those put to the sword by the invading Israelites. It was a totally avoidable tragedy. *23:19,20 23:21;24:16,17 24:14 31:8b*

O Lord, enable me to live
By standards which your love has set,
And those perceptions which you give,
Burn in my heart, lest I forget. PRAYER

TEMPTATION

READING NUMBERS 25:1–3
'While Israel was staying in Shittim, the men began to indulge in sexual immorality with Moabite women, who invited them to the sacrifices to their gods' (vv.1, 2a, NIV).

23:21–3

v.3

Judges 2:11–13

1 Kings 14:22–24

Jer 3:24;

11:13; 19:5

v.3b

Lev 19:2

FOLLOWING the high spiritual tone of Balaam's prophecies expressing God's determination that Israel should be blessed, and his pure, almost sublime view of Israel, we expected much more of his people than this. Instead of treating the Moabites as an enemy, the men indulged themselves with their women. It was but a step from that immoral relationship to offering sacrifices to the Baal of Peor, and God was angry with them for so doing.

Baal worship was a focal point for nature worship. Not least within the cult was the concept that fertility, of the ground, providing food, and of the body, providing children, was due to the action of Baal. Frequently, with Baal, the masculine god, was associated Ashtoreth, the female goddess of sexual love and fertility. Licentiousness, 'imitative magic' as John Gray describes it, was part of the worship, and to those who wished to legitimise lust, Baal worship must have had much to commend it. This naturistic religion was to plague Israel for centuries, and was one of the great evils Jeremiah opposed so strongly.

We are not surprised to read that 'the Lord's anger burned against them'. A Holy God cannot condone such behaviour. Because he is holy, we also are to be holy.

TO PONDER

Who serves a holy God
Must serve in holy ways;
No evil path be trod,
No evil given praise.
We serve a God who rules on high,
Who still in sovereign power is nigh.

A DRASTIC REMEDY

READING NUMBERS 25:4–18 (6–13)
'The Lord said to Moses, "Phinehas son of Eleazar, the son of Aaron, the priest, has turned my anger away from the Israelites; for he was as zealous as I am for my honour among them, so that in my zeal I did not put an end to them"' (vv.10–11, NIV).

THERE ARE TIMES when late twentieth-century views seem to distance us from some Scriptural events. The judgment on the leaders who sinned with the Moabite women and sacrificed to Baal appears extremely severe, with the following account of Zimri and Cozbi falling into the same category. But, if we try to evaluate the incidents in the context of 1000 BC rather than AD 2000 we shall begin to understand.

vv. 4,5
vv. 14,15

The nation was already involved in a series of major battles. Crucial to their success was faithfulness to the God who had chosen, liberated, disciplined and was about to prosper them. It was more than a mere affront to God that these men should surrender to the charms of Moabite women and sacrifice to their god. They broke at least four of the commandments, broke also the covenant God had made with Israel, and virtually denied God's right to sovereignty over them. Had their sin and rebellion spread, the entire undertaking would have been threatened. As in wartime, collaborators are shot both as punishment and to prevent further losses, so the offending Israelites were punished.

21:23–35

Exod 20:3,4,14,17
Exod 10:3–8

The priest, Phinehas, was applauded and rewarded because he shared God's sense of outrage at the behaviour of Zimri and Cozbi. His drastic action stopped the plague from spreading and helped Israel back to its priorities.

vv.6–13

Sin cannot lightly be ignored,
And drastic, painful is the cure,
But if God be his people's Lord,
His people must be pure.

TO PONDER

CONFIDENCE

READING NUMBERS 26:1–62 (1–4, 52–56)
"'Take a census of the whole Israelite community by families – all those twenty years old or more who are able to serve in the army of Israel'" (v.2, NIV).

Gen 12:2; cf
15:5

GOD HAD PROMISED that the people would multiply and flourish. We should hardly be surprised therefore, that the census reveals the number of men of military age standing on the threshold of the promised land, was but 1,820 fewer than the same census taken forty years earlier. This, in spite of the many disasters and the assertion that none other than Caleb and Joshua of the pilgrim people, would enter Canaan. God had virtually replaced the entire population in a period of forty years.

cf Num 2:32;
26:51
14:30

26:2
26:53
v.54

v.56; Joshua
18:5–10

There were two prime reasons for the census. The number of men eligible for military service had to be quantified, and the basis for the division of the land had to be established. A larger territory would be given to the larger tribes, but, presumably to avoid controversy between tribes of comparatively equal number, the final confirmation would be by lot.

25:1–13

To establish, before setting out for battle, the manner and means of distributing the land for settlement was a sign of confidence, with a further improvement in morale. Adding further to their confidence was the fact that the punishment, inflicted on the men who had compromised their inheritance by fraternising with the enemy, implied that God was on their side. They were assured of victory.

PRAISE

Round his standard ranging,
Victory is secure,
For his truth unchanging
Makes the triumph sure.
(Frances Ridley Havergal, SASB 707)

TWO EXCEPTIONS

READING NUMBERS 26:63–65
'Not one of them was left except Caleb son of Jephunneh and Joshua son of Nun' (v.65b, NIV).

THE PROMISE made concerning Caleb and Joshua was soon to be fulfilled; they, and they alone would represent the people who left Egypt some forty years earlier and at Kadesh, had stood on the borders of Canaan. Their survival and the key roles they were appointed to play, seem to suggest that God was emphasising faith, vision, and loyalty as dominant elements in following him. In spite of the many commandments given to regulate Israel, God was not merely seeking to institutionalise them as a nation, rather, he was concerned about their greater good. He desired to extend their spiritual horizons and to fulfil them in consequence.

14:30

13:26

God was looking for a people who would step into the unknown future with full confidence in him. Every day with God is a new day, full of opportunity, challenge, discovery and reward.

You are the God of new discovery,
Of new horizons and of newer ways,
The God whose style is serendipity,
Who lights our eyes and fills our hearts with praise.
You are the God of Israel's Exodus,
Of water from the rock, of flocks of quails,
Of safety through a desert perilous;
The God whose love and mercy never fails.

You are the God of constant pilgrimage,
Of barriers faced and barriers overcome,
Of turning deserts into pasturage,
Of turning minimum to maximum.

From your abundance we will draw new power
And walk your way each day and every hour.

WORDS OF PRAISE

READING 1 PETER 1:3–6
'Praise be to the God and Father of our Lord Jesus Christ! In his great mercy he has given us new birth into a living hope through the resurrection of Jesus Christ from the dead' (v.3, NIV).

THE EXCLAMATION MARK in our key verse is merited. Out of hearts full of wonder and gratitude we can praise our heavenly Father. Although our situation is different from those to whom Peter wrote, our more sophisticated societies are hardly less pagan than theirs. Modern 'gods' may have different names, different forms of 'worship', but they have their devotees and are as damaging to the soul as any ancient god. And, like the gods of old, they handle harshly the hopes of men and women.

Says Peter, we can praise God because in mercy (what else? we merit only judgment), adding 'We've been given a brand-new life and have everything to live for, including a future in heaven' as Eugene Peterson translates verse 3.

The resurrection of our Lord is the foundation of our hope. If his life had ended at Calvary, his story, had we heard it, would have touched our sentiments, but because there was a resurrection morning, his followers in every age have a living hope and a glorious inheritance in heaven.

> *Because he lives I can face tomorrow,*
> *Because he lives all fear is gone;*
> *Because I know he holds the future,*
> *And life is worth the living just because he lives.*
> (Gloria and William J. Gaither, H&H 7)

If the resurrection of our Lord guarantees the victory of right over wrong and the destiny of his people, we can rejoice in Christ who is our hope, and praise our heavenly Father.

PRAYER
> *Lord, let not opposition mute my praise,*
> *Or take me from your chosen ways,*
> *But let it strengthen and refine my days. Amen.*

PRAYER
SUBJECT
Christians who feel isolated.

FEMININE INTUITION

READING NUMBERS 27: 1–11

"'Why should our father's name disappear from his clan because he had no son? Give us property among our father's relatives'" (v.4, NIV).

LOGIC AND DETERMINATION supported the intuition of Zelophehad's daughters. According to the existing laws, sons only were allowed to inherit property, the firstborn son receiving a double portion. The prime reason was to keep the land within the family. A daughter had no such rights, she was dependent upon her father until marriage. On that happy day he provided a dowry, but afterwards she was the responsibility of her husband, their sons inheriting the property handed down through their father in due course. These forthright daughters failed to see why the land should be lost to their father's name and had tenacity enough to make their claim before Moses and the entire judiciary. Deut 21:15–17 Gen 34:12; cf Exod 22: 17 v.2

Zelophehad must have been a remarkable man. In an age when sons were preferred to daughters, he had no sons and five daughters. Even so, he named his last two daughters 'Counsel' and 'Delight'. Their determination would have pleased him. As a man unaffected by the rebellious Korah, his daughters argued that nothing should be lost to his family. God agreed with them and the law was amended accordingly 1 Sam 1:11 v.3; 16:1 v.4. v.6–11.

This event provides further evidence of the growing faith of the Israelites. Their confidence in God for victory over their enemies encouraged them to believe God's promises and to look forward to their inheritance.

> What shall I render to my God
> For all his mercy's store?
> I'll take the gifts he hath bestowed
> And humbly ask for more.
> AFFIRMATION
>
> (Charles Wesley SASB 23)

A MARK OF GREATNESS

READING NUMBERS 27:12–17
"'May the Lord . . . appoint a man over this community . . . so that the Lord's people will not be like sheep without a shepherd'" (vv.16,17, NIV).

v.13

v.12
20:2–13

v.17

MOSES' TIME was approaching when he would be gathered with his people, God shared this information as he directed Moses to climb to the top of Mount Nebo from which vantage point he could view the promised land. God also reminded him of the act of disobedience which occasioned this punishment, but such was the strength of Moses' relationship with God that he demurred not at all. Indeed, his concerns reflected no self-pity, simply total obedience and an overwhelming desire for the best good of his people.

14:20–23

Exod 32:31,32

12:8

With some justification we could draw from this incident the truth that frequently the costliness of some sin remains with us, even though the sin has long been forgiven, but that emphasis would cause us to overlook the sheer greatness of this man of God. Moses' sensitivity and tender-hearted concern are totally consistent with his behaviour in those earlier days when he stood between God and the people, pleading for them because of the enormity of their sin. Little wonder God loved him so much that he afforded him the privilege of a face-to-face relationship.

Matt 26:39

How God must long to observe a similar kind of selflessness in us. It is, of course, the selflessness of Christ who in the most trying situation, when some self-pity could have been expected, still prayed, 'Not as I will, but as you will'.

AFFIRMATION

Naught have we thou didst not give,
By thy life and grace we live,
Selfish aims do we forsake,
Service with our Lord to take.

(Charles Coller, SASB 532)

THE SUCCESSION ASSURED

READING NUMBERS 27:15–23
'So the Lord said to Moses, "Take Joshua son of Nun, a man in whom is the spirit, and lay your hand on him"' (v.18, NIV).

THE JOB DESCRIPTION Moses rehearsed before God in his prayer fitted Joshua admirably. It will be recalled that Joshua led the Israelites against the Amalekites at Rephidim to their first battle and first victory. Joshua became Moses' assistant, even ascending the holy mountain with him. No doubt because of his leadership skills and because he was the eyes and ears of his mentor, Joshua was one of those who explored the promised land. With Caleb, he brought a good report, only to be overruled by the other ten gloomy explorers. He was the obvious successor to Moses. `v.17` `Exod 17:8–14` `Exod 24:13` `13:8,16` `14:5–9`

Moses was commanded to give Joshua only 'some' of his authority. Unlike Moses, and unlike us, he was not to have 'face-to-face' contact with God, instead, he was to be subordinate to Eleazar, the high priest, who would obtain decisions for him by use of the Urim. The Urim, and Thummim were two somewhat mysterious objects carried in the high priest's breastplate. They were the sacred 'lot' thrown before the Lord at crucial times, to secure a decision. `v.20` `v.21`

Moses presented Joshua to the people as his successor, commissioning him as leader before the entire assembly by the laying on of hands. God had prepared his man, and the people, and the future looked bright. `vv.22,23`

> *Be strong in the grace of the Lord,* ENCOURAGEMENT
> *Be noble and upright and true,*
> *Be valiant for God and the right,*
> *Live daily your duty to do.*
> *Be strong! Be strong!*
> *And God will your courage renew.*
> (Walter Henry Windybank, SASB 679)

REFLECTIONS

READING NUMBERS 27:18–23
"'Give him some of your authority . . . He is to stand before Eleazar the
priest, who will obtain decisions for him . . .'" (vv. 20a,21a, NIV).

JOSHUA'S COMPLIANCE with the will of God leaves us
with the impression that he had no voice in this great
event. No doubt the idea was in his mind that this could
happen, but he would know enough about God not to
make any assumptions. He simply submitted himself to
WoL 25 Jan his destiny. We have already observed that Joshua did
not exactly replace Moses. He only had some of Moses'
authority; he had to stand before Eleazar and receive
vv. 20,21 answers to great problems. Clearly, he was not as
Moses was. Neither is there any evidence that Eleazar
v.22 construed his elevated role as a mandate for interfer-
ence. He too seemed to be content.

God has this lovely way of giving us gifts which enable
us to be happily employed in his service. Our differences
one from another can be quite obvious, but we each have
a crucial part to play in God's plan. The concept reaches
its peak in the New Testament with the strategy of the
people of God functioning as the body of Christ. The gifts
are given to 'prepare God's people for works of service'.
As we exercise our gifts so we build up the body of
Eph 4:7,11–16 Christ, achieving both unity and maturity and find personal fulfilment in the process.

God moves towards each of us with special grace. He
values us, stretches us, uses us and never, never
diminishes us. Our sense of well-being in his service
is important to him.

PRAYER
And so, with eyes that see anew
The task that thou to me hast given,
Let me my covenant renew
And bring a worthier gift to heaven.
(Miriam M. Richards, SASB 618)

READING NUMBERS 28:1ff; 29:1ff (28:1–8)
"'Give this command to the Israelites and say to them: 'See that you present to me at the appointed time the food for my offerings made by fire, as an aroma pleasing to me'"' (28:2, NIV).

THE COMMANDMENTS recorded in these two chapters reinforce further the expectation of entry into the promised land. After forty years in the wilderness with its lack of vegetation how beautiful the land of the Midianites must have appeared to them and even more beautiful the dream of the promised land must have been. They must have longed for land able to sustain livestock and provide them with crops and fruit. These commandments regarding sacrifices presuppose the prosperity of which they dreamed. To be able to offer lambs, grain, wine and cattle was an attractive prospect. *v. 3 v.5 v.7 v.11* The variety of food awaiting them must have stimulated their taste buds.

The sacrifices also presuppose the people's need of God. They needed the constant reminder that human nature with its sin and sinful disposition requires always the grace and favour of God. The use of the word 'atonement', with its connotation of bridging the gap *28:22, 30;* between sinful people and a holy God both emphasises *29:5, 11* and acknowledges that need.

Even so, there was pleasure and celebration. The burnt offerings produced an 'aroma pleasing to the Lord'. The Passover celebrated the escape from *29:2,6,8* Egypt. The Feast of Tabernacles celebrated the harvest *28:16,25; Deut* for seven exuberant days. The gloom of sin is never *16:1* distant, but neither is the joy of celebration. *29:12ff; Deut* *16:13–15*

PRAISE

    Christ is alive! His Spirit burns
      Through this and every future age,
   Till all creation lives and learns
     His joy, his justice, love and praise.
               (Brian Wren, SASB 142)

VOWS

READING NUMBERS 30:1–16 (1–8)
'When a man makes a vow to the Lord or takes an oath to bind himself by a pledge, he must not break his word but must do everything he said' (v.2, NIV).

ESPECIALLY IN TIMES of difficulty or stress, people have made vows to God. Jacob made his vow after his dramatic experience at Bethel as he escaped the wrath of his brother Esau. The condition he made, that God would protect him and provide for him, links him with generations of vow-makers. 'If God gets me out of this situation, I will go to church', 'If God helps me recover from this illness, I will give the rest of my life to him', etc, etc. The format spans the centuries.

Gen 28 20.

This Scripture gives guidance mainly in connection with the vows women make and reflects the low view held of women in those days. Only women who were widowed or divorced were entitled to make a vow which could not be nullified by a man, all others were subject to the approval of either father or husband. Happily, one of the great effects of the gospel has been to lift the position of women so that in Christ there is neither male nor female. We are all equal.

v.9
vv.3–8.

Gal 3:28

Jesus desired that we should not use God's name lightly, or indeed anything related to him, in vow-making. Our integrity should be such that our word should be enough. It should not be necessary for our word to be reinforced by a vow, such a requirement would mean that our plain words were suspect. Our Lord also stated that we will be judged by our words. Our word must be our bond.

Matt 5:34,35.

Matt 12:36,37.

TO PONDER

> *Forgive our sins as we forgive,*
> *You taught us, Lord, to pray;*
> *But you alone can grant us grace*
> *To live the words we say.*
> (Rosamond Eleanor Herklots, SASB 572)

WORDS OF PRAYER

READING PSALM 65:1–4
'Hearer of prayer, to you everyone should come' (v.2, REB).

'HEARER OF PRAYER' is a most beautiful name for God, it so admirably suits his role of Father. Does not a father encourage his children to come to him? Does he not listen to them and having heard the request, does he not endeavour to make an appropriate reply? (Matt 7:7–11) God takes his role as Father of mankind very seriously. In fact, Jesus, that other authority in hearing and answering prayer, who also encouraged us to pray (Matt 6:5–13), is on record as saying that if we believe, we will receive whatever we ask for in prayer (Matt 21:22).

It is a self-evident fact that everyone should approach God. Our needs are so great and our resources so small. The Psalmist points to the burden of our sinfulness (v.3). That is an overwhelming reason why we should go to God since he can forgive our sins. The Psalmist goes further, all who respond to him have the pleasure of being with him. What a tremendous privilege that is, and, being with him, God shares generously with us the good things he has to give (v.4).

PRAYER
How fitting is that name for you, O Lord,
For you are always near to answer prayer.
Your listening ear hears more than just the word,
You are aware of all the overtones of care.

Why you should bother, Lord, is mystery;
We often use our words thoughts to conceal,
Forgetting you can see with clarity
The gulf between our words and what we feel.

But you do hear, and you do understand
And to a ready answer you then move:
Since answers we observe on every hand
It's clear the answers but your hearing prove.

In my petitioning, Lord, just make me wise,
Then answers made will come as no surprise.

PRAYER SUBJECT
Those who are reluctant to pray.

MONDAY 30 JANUARY
VENGEANCE

READING NUMBERS 31:1–18
'So Moses said to the people, "Arm some of your men to go to war against the Midianites and to carry out the Lord's vengeance on them"' (v.3, NIV).

THE RUTHLESSNESS which accompanies a 'holy war' today should help us accept the 'total warfare' philosophy of the war against the Midianites. By describing the battle as 'the Lord's vengeance', the conflict had all the connotations of a holy war. Perhaps such a concept was necessary to help keep the nation pure. Regarding the women, Moses said, 'They were the ones who . . . were the means of turning the Israelites away from the Lord.'

v.16

v.49

Perhaps there was a need to glorify the conflict and victory, especially as there was not one Israelite casualty. But we who have seen death and destruction in war far beyond our forefathers imaginings, view triumphalism rather differently. In the cries of triumph we hear cries of grief, and believe our Lord mingles his tears with the grieving.

But now is not then. The dangers of religious assimilation were too great for Baal-worshippers and Israelites to coexist without loss to the purity of Israel, as subsequent history testifies. The battle was therefore pursued mercilessly. The one act of mercy, that of sparing the girls, was because they could not have been involved in the seduction of the men at Baal Peor. Difficult though it may be, we must try to understand the Israelite situation.

Judg 2:10–13

v.18

25:1–3

PRAYER

I have to serve you in the light today provides,
With all the insights given through the years;
Nor struggle over wars and genocides:
Those past events which hint that no one cares.
But in the light of history and Calvary,
The Garden Tomb and then of Pentecost,
I must believe you love humanity,
Your faithful people and the pagan lost.

CLEANSING

READING NUMBERS 31:19–24
"'All of you who have killed anyone or touched anyone who was killed must stay outside the camp seven days. On the third and seventh days you must purify yourselves and your captives'" (v.19, NIV).

INTOXICATED by their victory they may well have been, but they were still unclean and needed to be cleansed before they could be part of the community again. They had taken life. They had touched dead bodies, probably as they robbed them. They had much of which to be cleansed. This was, of course, a ritual cleansing but standing behind the ritual was the requirement to treat God as one who could not lightly be approached, and the lesser, but still important aspect of responsibility towards the community.

v.50

Exod 19:10–15; 30:19

Lev 15:31

But this cleansing could do little for the heart, with the vicious hatred some felt for their enemies; the newly discovered pleasure of inflicting pain; the ruthlessness of mortal combat; the greed of looting and the carelessness of war's consequences. Later in Israel's history, the Psalmist was to ask the questions, 'Who may ascend the hill of the Lord? Who may stand in his holy place?' and answer them so well, 'He who has clean hands and a pure heart.' In our day we have cause to be overwhelmed with gratitude for the cleansing of heart and mind which is ours through Christ.

Ps 24:3, 4a

1 John 1:7

Wash thou my hands, my heart, my mind,
Wash, if thou wilt, my past misdeeds,
Redeem the folly left behind,
The past which for thy mercy pleads.

PRAYER

Let me before thee, Lord, stand whole,
A tribute to thy power and grace,
Thy heartbeat sounding in my soul,
Thy love's light shining in my face.

JESUS THE HEALER

READING MATTHEW 14:34–36

'And when the men of that place recognised Jesus, they sent word to all the surrounding country. People brought all their sick to him' (v.35, NIV).

WoL 5 Nov

v. 34

v. 36

WE REFER again to Matthew's account of Jesus walking across the water to the disciples who were troubled by the strong wind and heavy seas, how Peter walked across the water to him and how, when Jesus entered the boat, the wind died and there was calm. This time our key verse relates to the landing at Gennesaret, and the response of the local population.

These three verses give us a picture of a world in great need. Sickness is common to every age and every society, but in communities where medical provision is scanty and hygiene virtually non-existent, the problems must have been immense. Because Jesus could heal diseases, the people spread the news and the crowds massed before him. Such was the throng that they quickly discovered even a touch of his cloak was sufficient to produce healing.

Our world today is as needy as it has been, and the people who come to him do so because they have heard that he meets human needs. How important it is for those of us who have felt his touch, to tell others of what he has done for us. Some may well find physical healing, but all who come will find a more enduring healing, that of the soul. Not many are attracted to Christ by our arguments, however thoughtful they may be, but the clear word of testimony, bearing witness to the way Christ has met our needs, has enormous drawing power.

AFFIRMATION

I want to tell you what the Lord can do,
What the Lord can do for you:
He can take your life as he did mine;
And make it anew.

(Sidney Edward Cox, SASB 335)

A CLASH OF PRINCIPLES

READING MATTHEW 15:1–9
"'Why do your disciples break the traditions of the elders? They don't wash their hands before they eat!'" (v.2, NIV)

THE QUESTION posed by the Pharisees and teachers of the law had consequences far greater than they imagined. They thought to discomfort Jesus, but only succeeded in discomforting themselves. More than that, Jesus used the occasion to highlight the fundamental difference between a religion which had become externalised, and true religion. The question the Pharisees asked was not simply related to hygiene. The tradition of the elders had decreed that there was a special way of washing the hands to avoid ceremonial uncleanness, and this ritual was not being followed by the disciples.

Jesus immediately responded by quoting the law related to the honouring of parents. He instanced the way in which some sons denied their parents honour and support by saying of their possessions they are 'Corban', that is, they are dedicated to the temple. By means of a tradition, therefore, they were able to break a specific commandment. Our Lord's quotation from Isaiah could not be more appropriate. *Mark 7:11,12 / v.3 / vv.8,9; Isa 29:13*

True religion is of the heart. While there are rituals which can be helpful, the danger is always that they can usurp the position of love in the heart: of personal religion. In this confrontation with the Pharisees any perceptive onlooker would be aware that the conflict could only continue unto death. There is no common ground between externalism and personal religion. *cf Col 2:20 / Hos 6:6; Rom 14:17*

> *O make and keep me clean,*
> *Spare not one lurking sin,*
> *So shall my life each day proclaim*
> *The Christ who dwells within.*
> (Albert Orsborn, SASB 494)

PRAYER

THE HEART'S SUPREMACY

READING MATTHEW 15:10–19
"'But the things that come out of the mouth come from the heart, and these make a man 'unclean'" (v.18, NIV).

vv.10,11,18–20

JESUS HEIGHTENED the conflict with the Pharisees by calling the crowd closer and began to explain the true nature of uncleanness. That which comes from within, thoughts and attitudes expressed in words or sins, render us unclean. Most, if not all, of his hearers would hold the traditional view that contact with a Gentile, with a body, with blood, with certain foods, etc, all requiring the ritual of cleansing, were the causes of uncleanness and lack of acceptance with God. But Jesus stood firmly with the prophets who expressed God's abhorrence of rituals when the heart was disobedient. Amos said it so powerfully, 'I hate, I despise your religious feasts; I cannot stand your assemblies. Even though you bring me burnt offerings and grain offerings, I will not accept them.'

Amos 5:21–4

v.12
v.13
v.14

The disciples were conscious of, and perhaps a little concerned at, the apparent resentment of the Pharisees, but Jesus was undismayed, prophesying that those things not of God's will, including people, would be appropriately dealt with by God. The Pharisees were but blind guides.

John 3:5–8

Since the heart is the source of rebellion against God, and since the rebellious heart cannot be controlled, Jesus came to change it. Nothing less than a new birth would do. God doesn't seem to have any problems with unwashed hands, but he treats an unclean heart with great seriousness.

PRAYER

I want, dear Lord, a heart that's true and clean,
A sunlit heart, with not a cloud between;
A heart like thine, a heart divine,
A heart as white as snow;
On me, dear Lord, a heart like this bestow.
(George Jackson, SASB 426)

A REMARKABLE MOTHER

READING MATTHEW 15:21–8
'A Canaanite woman from that vicinity came to him, crying out, "Lord, Son of David, have mercy on me! My daughter is suffering terribly from demon-possession"' (v.22, NIV).

AT THIS STAGE, the policy of Jesus was to concentrate on 'the lost sheep of Israel'. We assume that he and the disciples were in this region, north of Galilee, because he needed privacy and time to instruct his disciples. Somehow, this woman whose nation was one of Israel's sometime enemies, had heard of him and brought her daughter's need to him.

v.24

v.21

Jesus seemed disinclined to be helpful at first which was out of character with him, unless he was seeking to find and strengthen her faith. We note, for instance, that she qualified his Lordship by his human title, but when she knelt before him (with her growing faith seeing beyond the human to the divine?), she called him Lord, in a more definitive sense. It almost seems as though Jesus handled her rather roughly with the reference to the dogs, but Barclay points out that the word used for dogs was not the word for the vicious, uncared for, scavengers of the streets, but rather, the small, treasured, pet dog. We also assume that Jesus said it with a smile on his face, a twinkle in his eye, and a chuckle in his voice.

v.25

v.22

v.26

The mother, compassionate, cheerful and yet persistent, her faith growing by the moment, gave the answer which obviously delighted our Lord. And he who had difficulty in not rising to an obvious need, healed the girl from that moment.

> *Lowly paths our Lord has taken,*
> *And he proved by word and deed,*
> *For the lonely and forsaken*
> *There is grace beyond all need.*
> (Albert Orsborn, SASB 555)

TO PONDER

WORDS OF REINFORCEMENT

READING 1 PETER 1:3–9
**'These have come so that your faith – of greater worth than gold, which
perishes even though refined by fire – may be proved genuine and may
result in praise, glory and honour when Jesus Christ is revealed' (v.7, NIV).**

DIFFICULTIES AND TRIALS beset everyone, and how we confront
them helps to determine the kind of people we are. Peter sought to
be positive about the trials his readers were facing or about to face.
The trials were to prove their faith. By this assertion he turned what
could have been a negative and corrosive experience into a battle,
the goal being the further glory of our Lord. We take courage as we
link Peter's statement with that of Paul, 'No temptation has seized
you except what is common to man. And God is faithful; he will not
let you be tempted beyond what you can bear. But when you are
tempted, he will also provide a way out so that you can stand up
under it' (1 Cor 10:13). Whatever the trial, it need not overwhelm us.

Faith is not faith except it be tested. It can only be proved in the
crucible of life, and faith is fundamental to everything God wants to
do for us, and wants us to do for him (Heb 11:6). We are to live a life
of faith (Gal 5:6b).

Faith in the Lord Christ is the basis of our relationship with God
and with each other (1 John 3:23). Faith is more than a perspective,
although it is that. It is an anchor which holds us steady in the
storms of life; a sail which catches the winds of the Spirit; an inward
dynamic which drives us ever onward to new hope and achievement. Faith is 'being sure of what we hope for and certain of what
we do not see' (Heb 11:1). It is also a gift of God (Eph 2:8). By faith
we take the first faltering steps on our Christian pilgrimage; by it,
we sustain the challenge and the weariness of the journey, and by it
we enter heaven wherein we find our imperishable inheritance
(v.4).

PRAYER
*O Lord, the threshold of my pain is much too near,
And there are trials which my fainting heart would fear,
Grant me the faith to fight, to strive, to persevere.*

PRAYER
SUBJECT
Christians in daunting circumstances.

A MULTITUDE FED

READING MATTHEW 15:29–39
'. . . "I have compassion for these people . . . I do not want to send them away hungry . . ."' (v.32, NIV).

FROM THE REGIONS of Tyre and Sidon, Jesus led the disciples down to the eastern side of the sea of Galilee, an area largely populated by Gentiles. To make room for the crowd massing to see him, Jesus made his way up the slopes of the mountain, thereby establishing a suitable meeting place for human need and divine provision. What sorrows, frustrations and pain were represented by this gathering of sick people. But what happiness because of his healing touch.   v.21 v.29 v.30

Excitement and glad shouts of praise
Accompany Christ's healing ways,
As crippled people start to walk,
The life-long dumb begin to talk –
Spontaneously, the heart employs
Its liveliest gifts, to share its joys.

After three days of healing and rejoicing Jesus expressed concern about the long journeys people were about take, and their lack of food, a concern which led to another miracle of feeding. 'I do not want to send them away hungry', he said. He never sends us away spiritually hungry either. The only people who leave him unfed are those who choose to do so, such as the rich ruler and the Pharisees and Sadducees. To those who open their hearts to him, does he not become living bread and living water? The food for which our spirits crave, comes from him.   vv.33–38 v.32b 19:16–24 16:1,2 John 6:30–35 John 7:37–39

Christ is my meat, Christ is my drink,   AFFIRMATION
My medicine and health,
My peace, my strength, my joy, my crown,
My glory and my wealth.
(John Mason, SASB 346)

READING THE SIGNS

READING MATTHEW 16:1–4
'The Pharisees and Sadducees came to Jesus and tested him by asking him to show them a sign from heaven' (v.1, NIV).

INCREASINGLY, the religious leaders of the day perceived Jesus to be a threat to them. The more they saw of him the more sure they became that if they could not discredit him in the eyes of the people, thereby nullifying his influence, they would have to destroy him. Pharisees and Sadducees were strongly opposed to each other, but were completely united in their opposition to Jesus. For that to happen, Jesus had to be a most serious menace to them.

cf Acts 23:6–8

Our Lord's response was marvellously clear and yet totally infuriating to them. He instanced their ability to read the weather signs in the sky and their inability to read the signs of the times. Disdaining their request to provide a sign he repeated his earlier comment about the prophet Jonah. It will be recalled that the sign was not the great fish, but Jonah himself and his message.

vv.2–3

12:38–42 (WoL
13 Oct 94)

In effect, Jesus was saying that he was himself the sign. If they could not read in his character, teaching, insights, healings and his obviously special relationship with God, then they were blind, possibly incurably so. We recall that a Samaritan woman of dubious morality conversed with him, and concluded that he was probably the Christ; two blind men quickly seemed to identify him as Lord, but the men whose way of life should have made them sensitive to spiritual things, simply could not perceive him as the Christ.

John 4:29

9:27–31

PRAISE

O for a thousand tongues to sing
My great redeemer's praise;
The glories of my God and King,
The triumphs of his grace!

(Charles Wesley, SASB 64)

A MISUNDERSTANDING

READING MATTHEW 16:5–12
"'Be careful," Jesus said to them. "Be on your guard against the yeast of the Pharisees and Sadducees'" (v.6, NIV).

THE DISCIPLES had forgotten to take bread with them on this journey and our Lord's words about the yeast of the Pharisees seems to have increased their awareness of their failure. The incident helps pin-point our human tendency to allow an incident to become a crisis. Jesus obviously saw their discomfiture as they discussed the bread shortage between themselves, and put everything into perspective. It was a pity their faith could not rise to the occasion. Was Jesus not the one who had fed crowds of five thousand and four thousand respectively? By inference, a group of thirteen was a paltry problem. `v.5` `v.7` `14:13–21` `15:32–38`

Jesus was, however, greatly concerned that they should learn to identify the influences to which they were exposed and deal with them realistically. His illustration with the yeast, or leaven, was profoundly simple, yet effective. In Jewish thought, the yeast which, by its fermentation causes bread to rise, was a type of evil influence, hence grain offerings were to be made without yeast. Paul follows the corruption idea in his letter to the Corinthians. `vv.9, 10` `Lev 2:4–8` `1 Cor 5:6–8`

Jesus clearly concluded that the legalism of the Pharisees led to religious externalism; this opposed the idea of a personal faith. The Sadducees were politically motivated and very wealthy. Their temptation was to compromise their integrity for political gain. The leaven was worth avoiding.

> *O may I love like thee,*
> *In all thy footsteps tread!*
> *Thou hatest all iniquity,*
> *But nothing thou hast made.*
> (Charles Wesley, SASB 568)

PRAYER

A WATERSHED EXPERIENCE

READING MATTHEW 16:13–16

"'But what about you?" he asked. "Who do you say I am?" Simon Peter answered, "You are the Christ, the Son of the living God'" (vv.15,16, NIV).

CAESAREA PHILIPPI owes its strong place in Christian history to the fact that there, Peter affirmed Jesus was 'The Christ, the Son of the living God'. For the most obvious of reasons, Peter's statement is known as 'The Great Confession'. Almost lost in history is the shrine to the god Pan built on the mountain face, and the impressive mountain-top temple built in honour of Caesar, while from the foot of the mountain flows the stream which is one of the sources of the River Jordan.

The moment had come when it was essential that the disciples should be aware of the true nature of Jesus. From our vantage place in time we may feel that the disciples were slow to perceive the truth, so obvious to us, that Jesus was the Son of God, but then, hindsight almost always reveals perfect vision.

Luke 24:25

With the least threatening of questions Jesus paved the way for the great revelation. 'Who do people say the Son of Man is?' Back came the answers quickly, John the Baptist, Elijah, Jeremiah or another of the prophets. All highly regarded men. But Jesus was not unduly interested in the views of others on that day, those of his disciples were of far greater significance, therefore, with characteristic directness, he asked, 'Who do you say I am?' Sooner or later, he faces all of us with similar directness. Happy are those who can also make, 'The Great Confession'.

v.13

AFFIRMATION

You are the Christ,
In whom all heaven believes,
You are the Christ,
Through whom earth all heaven receives.

A CHANGE OF NAME

MATTHEW 16:13–18
'And I tell you that you are Peter, and on this rock I will build my church'
(v.18a, NIV).

THIS DRAMATIC revelation of the true nature of Jesus
and the renaming of Simon as Peter has been the focus of
much attention throughout the centuries. Obviously, the
moment when the divinity of Christ was declared was,   v.16
and has been since, a precious moment in the history of
God's people, but the comments regarding Peter and the
Church have also been of great historic value. Those who   vv.18,19
see Peter, the man, as the rock upon which the Church
has been founded, accept the fact that as the Bishop of
Rome, all of his successors have inherited his authority.
On this premise, millions of Catholics across the world
look to the Pope with awe and obedience.

Others, however, construe our Lord's words differently. Because we accept the fact that Jesus is the only
foundation stone of the Church, we look beyond Peter to   1 Cor 3:11;
the great truth he expressed about the Lordship of   10:4
Christ; seeing in Christ's divinity the foundational fact
of the Church. To us, the Church is built on this premise
that Jesus is the Christ. Our recognition of his Lordship
being the ground, the only ground, of our membership of
the universal Church. Important as Peter is, the truth he
articulated on that marvellous morning in Caesarea
Philippi is much greater.

> The church's one foundation   AFFIRMATION
>   Is Jesus Christ her Lord;
> She is his new creation
>   By water and the word;
> From heaven he came and sought her
>   To be his holy bride;
> With his own blood he bought her,
>   And for her life he died.
>   (Samuel John Stone, Hymns & Psalms 515)

INVINCIBILITY

READING MATTHEW 16:13–18
"'. . . you are Peter, and on this rock I will build my church, and the gates of Hades will not overcome it'" (v.18b, NIV).

THE CHURCH founded upon the Lordship of Jesus is unconquerable. Institutions have been known to last for many years,

> *But the Church of Jesus*
> *Constant will remain.*
> (Sabine Baring-Gould, SASB 690)

NIV mgn   All the forces of hell [Hades] will never be able to destroy a Church built on such a foundation as Jesus Christ. From an earthly angle the Church is well named as the Church Militant, and from the heavenly view as the Church Triumphant. Although less than perfect, and none know its imperfections more than its members, the Church is still indestructible.

Gates are usually accepted as passive in their roles. When closed, they keep people both out and in. If their strength is measured at all it must be by their ability to withstand an assault. But Jesus did not use the verb to withstand, he used a positive verb which means to overpower, to overcome, to prevail. To these gates he ascribed aggression, not defence, as though the gates represented the bounds of hell and the powers of evil were seeking to burst out of their limited territory, in much the same way as an advancing army keeps re-establishing its boundaries. The gates of hell will neither overpower the Church, nor will those gates be able to withstand the onward march of the soldiers of the cross.

AFFIRMATION

> *Satan never shall prevail,*
> *Thou, O Christ, shalt never fail;*
> *We who fight with thee shall win,*
> *Conquer over Hell and sin.*
> (Charles Coller, SASB 532)

READING 1 PETER 1:13–16
'But just as he who called you is holy, so be holy in all you do; for it is written: "Be holy, because I am holy"' (vv.15, 16, NIV).

THERE IS NO LIMIT to God's desires for his people. Peter was reminding the faithful in Asia Minor that they were not merely to be different, in so far as they had forsaken paganism for a living faith, but that the difference between them and their peers was to be unbelievably, incredibly great. God seems not to be over-interested in merely lifting human behaviour by a degree or two, but only in lifting it to the level of his own!

Imagine it. Slaves, those literally and legally fulfilling that low-status role (2:18), and those who once were slaves to sin (v.14; 2:1,11), being told that they were to be holy since their God is holy! In one sense, they would understand, because worshippers of idols behaved according to the way their god was defined, but in another sense they would see the impossibility of the instruction, because moral excellence, holiness, is not naturally attainable by fallen humanity.

Nevertheless, Peter affirmed the standard. Preceding this statement, he used the key words of grace and obedience (vv.13, 14). As we have seen (*WoL* 15 Jan), through God's grace we receive everything we need for victorious living, and by our obedience that grace is applied to our lives, giving us victory and making us Christlike. Our God is intensely practical!

He wills that I should holy be;
That holiness I long to feel,
That full divine conformity
To all my Saviour's righteous will.

On thee, O God, my soul is stayed,   PRAYER
And waits to prove thine utmost will;
The promise, by thy mercy made,
Thou canst, thou wilt in me fulfil.
(Charles Wesley, SASB 419)

For spiritual renewal   PRAYER SUBJECT

AUTHORITY

READING MATTHEW 16:17–20
'I will give you the keys of the kingdom of heaven' (v.19a, NIV).

v.18; 18:17

ONLY TWICE is the term church used in the gospels, each time being recorded in Matthew's gospel. In neither instance does our Lord have an institution in mind, but rather an assembly or congregation of people. In fact, the New Testament is remarkably consistent on this issue. The 'Church' is always people, a congregation 'called out' from the world to belong to Christ. Inevitably, with the passage of time and the need to accommodate the growing numbers of believers, venues had to be established, worship would evolve and service be regulated, but, even so, the Church is people, not buildings or an institution. It is an organism, not an organisation.

Acts 2:41

Acts 10:23b–48

Acts 15:1ff

[vv.7–11] Acts 8:4–8, 26–38

Acts 13:46–48

The keys of the kingdom, although given to Peter and used by him, quickly passed to the worshipping and witnessing body of believers. Peter demonstrated his stewardship of the keys on the day of Pentecost. Following his sermon on that day, 3,000 people entered the kingdom. The Holy Spirit also used Peter in the house of Cornelius to open the door of the kingdom to the Gentiles, and his witness was crucial at the Council of Jerusalem which established the place of Gentiles in the Church. But others confirmed that they too held this all-important key, not least Philip, Paul and Barnabas.

It is true to say that opening the door of the kingdom, and responsibility for discipline within the Church, v.19b are the privileges of the Church, the people who are Christ's Body.

PRAYER

> O lead me, Lord, that I may lead
> The wandering and the wavering feet;
> O feed me, Lord, that I may feed
> Thy hungering ones with manna sweet.
>   (Frances Ridley Havergal, SASB 612)

THE WAY OF SUFFERING

READING MATTHEW 16:21
'From that time on Jesus began to explain to his disciples that he must go to Jerusalem and suffer many things' (v.21a, NIV).

A SUFFERING MESSIAH was not a picture which readily commended itself to the Jewish mind. Rather, they had the idea of a militant figure who, with a flashing, righteous sword and a burning nationalism, would lead Israel to battle against the occupying Romans. The Jewish expectation was of a greater than King David who would restore their boundaries, independence and prosperity, but Jesus was interpreting his ministry in the light of Isaiah's remarkable prophecy of the Suffering Servant of the Lord.

cf Luke 24:21

Isa 52:13–53:12

Jesus was to suffer in Jerusalem. Because it was the capital, King David's city, the centre of the Jewish faith and place of constant sacrifice for the sins of the people, Jerusalem was a logical venue. In the city where for centuries animals had been the sacrifice for sin, Jesus made the complete sacrifice.

Heb 10:8–14

But Christ, the heavenly Lamb,
    Takes all our sins away.

                              (Isaac Watts, SASB 120)

Jesus was to suffer at the hands of the religious leaders of the day: those who had already received scriptural light to walk by, who were stewards of a remarkable religious history and tradition, and had become so blinkered by their assets that they could not recognise truth, and crucified the Christ. They should have known so much better than to do that.

The suffering servant he became,
    Yea more; in loneliness and loss
He bore for me in grief and shame,
    A crown of thorns, a heavy cross.
                    (Edward Henry Joy, SASB 451)

TO PONDER

OPPOSING VALUES

READING MATTHEW 16:21–3
'. . . your outlook is not God's but man's' (v.23b, JM).

Isa 55:8

1 Cor 1:10–
2:16

1 Cor 7:1–39

Acts 15:36–40

WE NEED to be reminded from time to time that our thought processes do not naturally coincide with the thought processes of God. On behalf of God, Isaiah stated confidently, 'For my thoughts are not your thoughts, neither are your ways my ways.' In his words to the Corinthians which included the statement that Christ was the wisdom and power of God, Paul rightly claimed to have the mind of Christ. He was less sure when dealing with marriage, concluding that he thought he had the Spirit of God. With hindsight he would probably have confessed that, in his conflict with Barnabas over Mark, he was not really on God's wavelength, even did not always have God's outlook.

Matt 4:1–11

The well-meaning Peter, passing judgment on Christ's statement regarding his future suffering, death and resurrection, revealed all too clearly that he had the wrong perspective. The redemption of sinful mankind called for more than a mere formula along the lines of the reconciliation documents beloved by peace-seeking commissions; it required a costly, reconciling act, demanding suffering and death before the triumph of the resurrection could be enjoyed. Jesus had already put aside Satan's temptations and in Peter's words, implying that there was an easier route, he heard the voice of the tempter again. Sin is not that easily dealt with.

TO PONDER

Our sin was ever thus:
A hateful thing, a shame inglorious,
A cause of pain, distress to me,
A cause of pain, distress to thee.
Lord, lift me up, let me behold
Thy mercies great and manifold,
And from thy nail-pierced, open hand
Receive the peace thy love has planned.

A CONDITION OF DISCIPLESHIP

READING MATTHEW 16:24
'Then Jesus said to his disciples, "If anyone would come after me, he must deny himself and take up his cross and follow me"' (v.24, NIV).

OLD TESTAMENT CONCEPTS tended to cultivate the idea that obedience to God and prosperity went hand in hand, but Jesus makes it clear that discipleship carries with it a breathtaking identification with himself. Even today, the common supposition may well be that comfort and plenty are the lot of the faithful, but that human expectation does not and has never, matched our Lord's concept. *Exod 23:25; Isa 30:19–26; Mal 3:10*

As Jesus denied himself, surrendering totally to the will of his heavenly Father, so he requires submission from us. The prayer Jesus taught his disciples and which is ours by right of discipleship, 'Your kingdom come, your will be done on earth as it is in heaven', implies minimum comfort but maximum fulfilment. We have no rights to our own way, only the privileges and joys associated with God's way. *Matt 26:39* *Matt 6:10*

So close to us is this spirit of self-denial that we are to perceive the cross as a present, daily reality. Whatever each day requires of us in the way of surrender to God, we are to give willingly and, surely, happily. *Luke 9:23*

The trivial round, the common task,
Will furnish all we ought to ask;
Room to deny ourselves, a road
To bring us daily nearer God.
(John Keble, SASB 668)

Help me, O Lord, your values to accept, PRAYER
The pull of ease to steadfastly defy;
To fix my eyes on you and on your cross,
And all my selfish thoughts and claims deny.

FINDERS AND LOSERS

READING MATTHEW 16:25
'For whoever wants to save his life will lose it, but whoever loses his life for me will find it' (v.25, NIV).

19: 16–24

THE INSTINCT of self-preservation is enormously strong within us. Without it, life would be shorn of that brand of tenacity which has ennobled mankind, even though the same instinct has been responsible for some quite despicable behaviour. But in this verse, Jesus is saying that our natural tendency to preserve and improve ourselves will only produce the opposite result. The rich young man who felt he had too much to lose by following Christ is a scriptural illustration of that truth. Our own experience also supports our Lord's words. Do we not know those whose lives have become smaller, less attractive and less valuable as they concentrated on their own concerns, denying themselves the pleasure and spiritual growth which follows living for others.

By implication, Jesus suggests that it is possible to lose one's life in a variety of ways. Our newspapers supply some of the headings: money, drugs, sexual immorality or some other cause. However, it is only those who lose their lives for Jesus, who will find themselves. Human nature, marred by its inheritance, countless temptations and unwise decisions, presents a self helpless and lost. Only in Christ, through his gift of new life and the indwelling of his Spirit, can we live truly free, unselfish, loving and fulfilled lives.

PRAYER

If I but give myself to thee,
Surrender to thee every right,
Depend upon thee utterly,
Live in thy way and in thy light;
Then will I true fulfilment know,
My true self in Christ's own self find,
In his blessed likeness daily grow,
My life expressive of his mind.

A BAD DEAL

READING MATTHEW 16:26
'What good will it be for a man if he gains the whole world, yet forfeits his soul? Or what can a man give in exchange for his soul?' (v.26, NIV)

WITH PROFOUND SIMPLICITY our Lord emphasises the value of the human soul, and we are left pondering on the ease with which so priceless and irreplaceable a treasure can be traded for such tawdry things and experiences.

Beware my soul!
I will sell thee for less than thou art worth.
Though thou art valuable beyond all price
There are some things on this our transient earth
I would yield thee for, and count no sacrifice.

People have concentrated on a variety of pursuits, not always knowing they have placed their souls in jeopardy. Some of the objectives are the more obvious grosser indulgences, but some are those with which ordinary people are totally familiar such as sport, hobbies, home, comfort, work, to name but a few. Esau sold his birthright for a bowl of red stew, Demas sold his soul for love of the world; clearly, it is not too hard a thing to do.

Gen 25:29–34
2 Tim 4:10

Our Lord pin-points the folly of exchanging the soul for an impermanent treasure or pleasure. Life at its longest is still short, especially in the light of eternity. Our life's investment ought never to be in temporary things; as a pilgrim people our real treasures are to be in heaven.

Matt 6:19–24

When I survey the wondrous cross
On which the Prince of Glory died,
My richest gain I count but loss,
And pour contempt on all my pride.

AFFIRMATION

(Isaac Watts, SASB 136)

WORDS OF ADORATION

READING 1 PETER 1:17–25
'You call him Father, when you pray to God, who judges all people by the same standard . . . so then, spend the rest of your lives here on earth in reverence for him' (v.17, GNB).

WE REVERENCE and adore our heavenly Father. Our chosen verse stimulates feelings of awe because God, who is judge of all, allows us to call him Father. When we pray, it is not with words expressive of our fear, but words expressive of our love and adoration. God does not cease to be the judge of all the earth, but Jesus encouraged us to call him Father (Matt 6:8–13) and his warm response assures us that we have not been misled.

> *We adore thee, heavenly Father,*
> *And we thank thee, heavenly Father,*
> *And we praise thee, heavenly Father,*
> *As we pray.*
>
> (John Gowans, SASB 192)

We adore, thank and praise him, because he redeemed us from the sterile life which is our natural heritage (v.18). Indeed, God's care for a fallen world is such that his Son was chosen to be the Lamb of sacrifice, 'without blemish or defect', from before the creation of the world (vv.19,20). Human sin did not take God by surprise and in love he provided a costly remedy.

> *Precious Lamb by God appointed,*
> *All our sins on thee were laid;*
> *By almighty love anointed,*
> *Thou hast full atonement made.*
>
> (John Bakewell, SASB 109)

By the gift of Jesus, God gave us the surest of grounds for believing in him (v.21). It helps explain why across the world men and women are singing hymns of adoration.

PRAYER
> *Joyful, joyful, we adore thee,*
> *God of glory, Lord of love.*
>
> (Henry van Dyke, SASB 10)

PRAYER SUBJECT
> *Abused and disadvantaged children.*

TWO PROMISES

READING MATTHEW 16:27–8
'For the Son of Man is going to come . . .' (v.27a, NIV)

FOLLOWING the stern words related to discipleship with
the emphasis on self-denial and cross-bearing, and his   v.24
paradoxical statement about losing and saving one's
life, Jesus made reference to two 'comings'. The first   v.25
was a promise of judgment for all. We are accountable
for our actions and we shall be rewarded accordingly.   v.27
Although we have been granted freedom to make our
own choices in life, those choices are not without
significant consequences.   2.Cor 5:10

The second promise was to be fulfilled much earlier   v.28
than could have been imagined. All too soon, the
suffering Jesus had spoken of became true. And cruelly   v.21
though the soldiers 'crowned' him, it was his coronation: 27:27–31
and from his cross the Son of Man, in a very real sense
began to reign.

> *Sinners in derision crowned him,*
> *Mocking thus the Saviour's claim;*
> *Saints and angels crowd around him,*
> *Own his title, praise his name.*
> (Thomas Kelly, SASB 147)

Was not Pilate's unintentional prophecy of declaring the
kingship of Jesus on the cross itself, in the three major
languages of the day, suggestive of the universal appli-   John 19:19,20
cation of that title, soon also to be gloriously realised?
Did not Jesus come in power to establish his kingdom
when the Holy Spirit came at Pentecost? And did not the   Acts 2:1–13
news of his kingship spread quickly throughout the world
and has it not continued to do so ever since?

> *Crown him, crown him!*   PRAISE
> *Spread abroad the victor's fame!*
> (Thomas Kelly, SASB 147)

THE TRANSFIGURATION

READING MATTHEW 17:1,2
'After six days Jesus took with him Peter, James and John the brother of James, and led them up a high mountain by themselves' (v.1, NIV).

THE MOUNTAIN was probably Mount Hermon even though a tradition exists declaring that the mountain was Tabor. Against Tabor is the fact that it was capped by a great fortress making it an unlikely place for such a revelation. Supportive of Hermon was its proximity to Caesarea Philippi. A reflective, teaching journey of some six days makes Hermon the most likely venue.

Luke 9:28

Luke makes the point that Jesus retired to the mountain with the disciples in order to pray, the transfiguration taking place as he prayed. Our Lord was essentially a man of prayer, but we know that he always sought his heavenly Father's guidance when faced with the larger issues of his ministry, and this was one such occasion.

cf Luke 6:12

16:21

We make the assumption that after Peter's dramatic insight concerning his Messiahship, and the need to press on to Jerusalem, there to suffer and die, Jesus needed further confirmation from God that his strategy was correct.

Jesus received that confirmation overwhelmingly. As he communed his body underwent a dramatic change. It was as though his earthly body surrendered to his divinity which radiated a heavenly glory. Literally, he was transfigured.

TO PONDER

Did not his garments glow with light,
His flesh with heavenly glory shine,
God's voice assure him, he was right,
He was God's Son: he was divine?
And did not Christ descend that hill
Its glory in his memory,
To find a greater glory still
On lonely, sin-swept Calvary?

MOUNTAIN-TOP COMPANIONS

READING MATTHEW 17:1–3
'Just then there appeared before them Moses and Elijah, talking with Jesus' (v.3, NIV).

TWO GREAT FIGURES from the past came from the eternal world to share these moments with Jesus. We can understand why Moses should be one because of his outstanding qualities of leadership and goodness. Moses had also prophesied of Christ, but we need to speculate a little more regarding the choice of Elijah. He was, of course, one of the earliest prophets, who holds an exalted place in Jewish history, but it was commonly believed that Elijah would appear to prepare the way for the Messiah. Jesus himself confirmed this, revealing that in John the Baptist the expectation had been fulfilled.

Num 12:6–8
Acts 3:22;
Deut 18:18

Mal 4:5

vv.10–13

Moses and Elijah talked with Jesus about his 'decease' or his 'departure'. The Greek word used was the appropriate and imaginative word 'exodus'. Our Lord was to make no ordinary passage from this world. It is of interest that neither Moses nor Elijah went to heaven in an ordinary kind of way either.

Luke 9:31, (AV)
9:31 (NIV);
2 Pet 1:15

Deut 34:5,6;

Did these two men, standing with Jesus on a hillside tell him about that other hill where two quite different men would be with him? One who would verbally abuse him, and the other who would take a believing, almost prophetic, role by asking, 'Jesus, remember me when you come into your kingdom: 'But Moses and Elijah would reassure Jesus that his heavenly Father would be with him, regardless of his feelings on that day.

2 Kings 2:9–12

Luke 23:42

Matt 27:45

God is not absent from this world of ours,
Nor stands he on the sidelines of our field,
But he is with us in our testing hours
Combating evil; forcing it to yield.
Our God is with us! Had we eyes to see
We would perceive his glorious majesty.

PRAISE

MOMENTS TO SAVOUR

READING MATTHEW 17:1–4
'Peter said to Jesus, "Lord, it is good for us to be here. If you wish, I will put up three shelters – one for you, one for Moses and one for Elijah"' (v.4, NIV).

SOME EXPERIENCES in life are of such a quality that they are to be caught, held on to for as long as possible, and savoured ever afterwards. Some of us recall special moments of communion with God when time seemed to stand still, and, while we have been experiencing the wonder of the encounter, we have been willing the experience to persist. It seems to have been so with the disciples at the transfiguration of our Lord.

Peter wanted to give permanence to the occasion by suggesting that he build shelters for Jesus, Moses and Elijah. Presumably, the three disciples would wait upon Jesus and his two extra-terrestrial guests. However, as Peter spoke, enjoying the glory they were seeing, an even greater glory came upon them. It was the Shekinah glory! The cloud of glory through which God revealed himself.

v.5a

The Israelites knew much of this. Had not God led them from Egypt in a pillar of cloud by day and of fire by night? Was not God in the cloud, with Moses when the commandments were given? Did not the cloud cover the Tent of Meeting and the glory of the Lord fill the first tabernacle? When Solomon dedicated the temple he had built was it not the same cloud and glory which filled the temple? And then, God spoke! Quite understandably, the disciples were overwhelmed and fell on their faces.

Exodus 13:21,22
Exodus 34:5
Exodus 40:34,35
2 Chron 5:13,14
v.5b, v.6

HOPE

And beyond await the heights of rapture
Where all earthly joys, transcended, fade
In the glory of the Saviour's presence,
In the home eternal he has made.

(Lily Sampson, SASB 711)

FEAR AND REASSURANCE

READING MATTHEW 17:5–7
**'But Jesus came and touched them. "Get up," he said. "Don't be afraid"'
(v.7, NIV).**

GOD'S VOICE was not always the most welcome sound
to the Israelites. During the giving of the Law the people
had kept their distance from the mountain and they said
to Moses, 'Speak to us yourself and we will listen. But do
not have God speak to us or we will die.' They also   Exod 20:18–20
believed that no one could see God's face and live. With   Exod 33:20
a historical background of that nature, it is understandable that when the Shekinah glory surrounded Peter,
James and John, and God spoke out of the cloud, that
they should be overwhelmed. We would have thought
with awe and wonder, but the Scripture says they were
terrified. Their fear linked them closely with their na-   v.6
tion's roots.

The situation had not overwhelmed their master. With
tenderness and sensitivity he approached them and
touched them. Our Christ does not stand back from us,
disdaining to make contact with us. He is a highly tactile
Lord: willing to touch the poor, even lepers if need be.
And have not we felt his touch at times upon our souls?   Matt 8:1–3

> *Was ever touch like yours, dear Lord?*
> *A strength-imparting, loving touch*
> *Through which new confidence is poured.*
> *It means so much, so very much.*

Then Jesus spoke. They were not to lie, fearfully, on the
ground but to rise to their feet as he banished their fears.

> *Was ever word like yours, Lord, heard*   PRAISE
> *In all creation's broadest span?*
> *A word by which our hopes are stirred;*
> *Which speaks the love of God to man.*

THE EVER-PRESENT CHRIST

READING MATTHEW 17:5–8
'And when they had lifted up their eyes, they saw no one but Jesus only' (v.8, NKJV).

WE DO NOT KNOW how long Moses and Elijah were with Jesus. We assume that when heaven and earth come together, when timelessness breaks into the realm of time, a moment of time could easily be expanded without human awareness. However, after God had spoken and the disciples had fallen on their faces in fear, when they looked up they saw 'no one but Jesus only'.

v.3

Moses and Elijah had words only for Jesus. Separated as they were by history, they had nothing to say to the disciples. Important though Moses and Elijah were, and acknowledging history's debt to them, the disciples could still manage without them. But they could not manage without Jesus.

Jesus was the encouraging one; the essential one; the eternal one. The great figures of history belong to history, they have their important places: but Jesus transcends time: he is above history, and is perpetually relevant.

John 1:1–14
Matt 28:20b.

Happy are those who, being anxious, look up and see Jesus only. Does not his presence give perspective to our fears and distresses? In the lonely places, geographical, emotional or spiritual, does not his presence assure us of resources?

PRAYER

Let nothing on this earth, Lord,
And naught from heaven above,
Obscure the sight I have, Lord,
Of you in all your love.

Let me but see you clearly,
See you, and you alone,
Maintain your face in focus
Wherein God's face is shown.

WORDS OF GRACE

READING 1 PETER 1:22–5
'For you have been born again, not of perishable seed, but of imperishable'
(v.23, NIV).

THE DIFFERENCE between being a pagan and a child of God is so dramatic, revolutionary, life-changing, that it can only be described as being 'born again'. John, in his prologue, makes the same point as Peter, that the new birth is not of natural, but of divine will and energy (John 1:13), and it was Jesus who bewildered Nicodemus with the assertion that only a new birth qualified people to enter the Kingdom of God (John 3:3–8).

While we do not cease to be a part of our natural family, we acquire a new family, the family of God, to whom we lovingly relate. With sensible realism, Kenneth Taylor brings Peter's word up to date: 'Now you can have real love for everyone because your souls have been cleansed . . . so see to it that you really do love each other warmly, with all your hearts' (v.21, LB). This kind of warm, pure, supportive, unconditional love is the natural expression of this new life in Christ.

James Moffatt, commenting on this new birth, with the resultant new life, makes the perceptive comment that we should 'let its instincts have full play'. We know well the instincts of ordinary people. Have we not experience of those drives and desires classified as normal in our society, some of which are creative and noble, while others are much less so.

Does not the heart leap at the prospect of those who are filled with the love of Christ allowing all those basic drives and desires to find expression? The instincts of a heart reborn by the Spirit can be none other than the instincts of our Lord himself. In realistic terms are not those instincts the ones God would classify as normal?

PRAYER

Express yourself, O Christ, in me,
By love, by generosity,
By all the virtues you possess;
Lord, through my life, your life express.

PRAYER
SUBJECT

Hospital chaplains.

A MOUNTAIN VIEW

READING MATTHEW 17:1–13
'. . . Jesus . . . led them up a high mountain . . .' (v.1, NIV).

TODAY we look back over this mountain-top experience of our Lord and reflect upon mountain-top experiences in the lives of the two other eminent people who shared this occasion with him.

Exodus 19:20

It was to the top of Mount Sinai that God called Moses to receive instructions from him. On that same mountain top, Moses received the second set of tablets on which the Law was written and when he came down, the glory of God was shining on his face. Of this radiance Moses was quite unaware, but it was perhaps an experience not unlike that of our Lord, even if to a lesser degree.

Exodus 34:1–7
Exodus 34:29–35

1 Kgs 19:1–13

Like Moses, Elijah also had a number of special experiences on mountains. One which calls for attention relates to a time when he was greatly dispirited because Jezebel, the pagan wife of King Ahab, was determined to kill him. Elijah fled for his life, arriving at Mount Horeb after a forty day's journey. As Moses had been granted a knowledge of the presence of God, so Elijah was given his own distinctive experience. God came to him, not in a fierce wind, or a subsequent earthquake, nor the fire which followed, but in a gentle whisper.

To these men was given the privilege of meeting the Christ on Mount Hermon. Both of them knew the loneliness of discipleship and leadership, but both also knew the grace and the glory of God.

AFFIRMATION

Christ also knows the lonely place,
Where isolation dwells,
And makes available his grace
From ever-present wells.

He comes with tenderness of speech
The waiting soul to bless,
And meets with love our faltering reach
To banish our distress.

READING MATTHEW 17:14–16
'When they came to the crowd, a man approached Jesus and knelt before him. "Lord, have mercy on my son," he said' (vv.14,15a, NIV).

NOT UNEXPECTEDLY, as Jesus and the three disciples returned to the valley they were immediately faced with the harsh realities of life. How they must have longed to remain on the mountain, but how glad they were to know that Jesus was going down into the valley with them. Joseph A. Robinson articulates this:

v.4

SASB 154

> 'Tis good, Lord, to be here,
>   Yet we may not remain;
> But, since thou bidst us leave the mount,
>   Come with us to the plain.

Although the pattern of moving from a mountain-top experience, with its exultation, to the threatening valley experience, seems well established, Jesus still remains with his people.

It was the boy's father who detached himself from the crowd to make an appeal to Jesus. A child's problem is a parent's problem and this father was true to the highest standards of fatherhood. Jesus would value that. 'Like as a father pitieth his children, so the Lord pitieth them that fear him.' The compassion of the human father relates to the divine compassion. Jesus would have responded positively but the quality of the father's love was an added desirable factor.

Ps 103:13 (AV)

PRAISE

> If human hearts are often tender,
>   And human minds can pity know,
> If human love is touched with splendour,
>   And human hands compassion show,

> Then how much more shall God our Father
>   Our wants supply, and none deny!
>   (John Gowans, SASB 50)

WEDNESDAY 1 MARCH
THE REALITY OF FAILURE

READING MATTHEW 17: 14–19
'I brought him to your disciples, but they could not heal him' (v.16, NIV).

WITH HIGH HOPES the father had brought his son to the disciples who had found the healing task beyond their ability. This failure was slightly surprising because Jesus had earlier given them the authority and power both to preach, and to heal every disease and sickness.

10:1.

Perhaps the disciples were daunted by the size of the task facing them and believed it was beyond their powers. It was providential that Jesus and his three disciples arrived on the scene at that very moment.

v.14, SASB 16

Robert Grant's line suited the disciples and also fits us:

Frail children of dust and feeble as frail.

If only the disciples had been more like their master! If only we were more like him also! It is God's intention that we should be more like our Lord and that goal is also our desire, but so often when the time of testing comes, instead of showing the authority and power which had been invested in us, we simply demonstrate that we are still flawed. For obvious reasons, the world, like the

v.15

epileptic boy's father, has more confidence in our Lord than in his disciples.

Our world is a frenzied place at times, seemingly bent on self-destruction, throwing itself into the fires of aggression, anarchy and civil war; or with wilful abandon plunging into the deep waters of addiction, indulgence and selfishness. How desperately it needs the Church and the Church's master!

PRAYER

O Lord, grant me the power to reach
And touch lost souls with healing hand.
Dispel my groundless doubts, and teach
Me how to help another stand.

THE REASON FOR FAILURE

READING MATTHEW 17:19–21
'Then the disciples came to Jesus in private and asked, "Why couldn't we drive it out"' (v.19, NIV)

THE DISCIPLE'S QUESTION was valid and helpful. They had obviously tried to dismiss the demon which possessed the boy and were smarting under the rebuke of their failure. Probably they had followed the procedures Jesus had used and taught them, and yet the boy's illness remained to the father's distress and their discomfiture. Our Lord's answer was simple and basic: they had insufficient faith. vv.14–16
v.20a

We make the assumption that the disciples had followed the methods of healing Jesus had employed, but they were to learn that the method without the dynamic of faith was of little value. This truth can be generalised; Christian procedures, rituals or ceremonies are of little worth without the all-essential quality of faith.

When we refer to the Christian faith we are not referring to the faith of a Christian, but rather to the set of spiritual propositions which identify a person of Christian persuasion. But the faith Jesus spoke of to the disciples was much more personal than that. It was a trust in himself as Lord and Master, a trust which helped to facilitate miracle working, such as the healing of the centurion's servant, or the healing of the man brought to Jesus on a stretcher by his four friends. Or that special trust which enabled, and still enables, people to perform remarkable deeds on his behalf. Acts 6:7

Matt 8:5–13,
Mark 2:1–12;
cf Matt 13:58
Luke 10:18;
John 14:12
PRAYER

> *I want the faith of God,*
> *Great mountains to remove,*
> *Full confidence in Jesus' blood,*
> *The faith that works by love.*
> (William James Pearson, SASB 733)

THE MYSTERY OF FAITH

READING MATTHEW 17:14–20
"'Why couldn't we drive it out?" He replied, "Because you have so little faith . . .'" (vv.19b,20a,NIV)

v.16

v.20b

THE DISCIPLES were nonplussed and, no doubt, not a little hurt by their failure to heal the epileptic boy. Their hearts would have been stirred by the obvious plight of the boy and the love of his father. They would have enjoyed being the instruments of healing, instead, their inadequacies were exposed. Jesus pin-pointed their problem by stating that they lacked faith, affirming that if they had sufficient faith they would move mountains. Even faith, as small as a mustard seed, would produce miraculous results. By inference, their faith did not even measure up to the smallest of Israel's seeds.

Faith is not a natural quality to mankind. True, from our earliest days with our parents we learn to trust and we gradually extend the area of that trustfulness, but that is not the trust, the humanly-generated faith, to which Jesus was referring. Rather, it was to a faith in himself as the Christ, with all the overtones of the world from which he had come, and those other-worldly powers which alone can achieve great things here, to which he was referring. This faith is of heaven, not of earth. Faith is a gift, but this aspect of it enables us to press beyond the barriers which hold us in our world, and makes available to us, vast, undreamed-of resources.

Eph 2:8

PRAYER

O give me faith, Lord,
Faith to see beyond each circumstance,
Faith to grasp my true inheritance,
Faith to let my doubting heart be stirred.

O give me faith, Lord,
Faith to be, and faith to nobly act,
Faith to turn my vision into fact,
Faith that hope and love be ever spurred.

THE ACHIEVEMENTS OF FAITH

READING MATTHEW 17:14–20
'. . . If you have faith as small as a mustard seed, you can say to this mountain, "Move from here to there" and it will move. Nothing will be impossible for you' (v.20, NIV).

THE MUSTARD SEED was one of the smallest of seeds in Palestine and while it never grew into a huge tree, its growth, in relationship to its size, was sufficient to impress people. Our Lord elsewhere referred to the birds happy to perch on its branches, and hide in its shade. Jesus used the mustard seed as an illustration of how even a little faith can produce a substantial result.   Mark 4:31,32

To the man or woman of faith, said Jesus, 'Nothing is impossible.' He would not mean that quite literally a mountain could be moved from here to there. A handful of people of faith exercising their gift could confuse us greatly by moving mountains around more or less at will! Our Lord was simply indicating how difficulties of mountainous proportions could be removed.

The problems facing Paul and Silas in Philippi were enormous, with no obvious solution in sight, but the obstacles yielded to faith and confidence, and the   Acts 16:16–40 church, which possibly became Paul's favourite church, was established. In like manner, those men   Phil 4:10–19 and women of faith who have planted new churches in the former USSR have faced seemingly unbreachable barriers, and have won through by faith.

> All things are possible to God,   AFFIRMATION
>   To Christ, the power of God in man,
> To me, when I am all renewed,
>   When I in Christ am formed again,
> And witness, from all sin set free,
> All things are possible to me.
> (Charles Wesley, SASB 407)

WORDS OF REINFORCEMENT

READING 1 PETER 2:1–3
'As newborn babes, desire the pure milk of the word, that you may grow thereby' (v.2, RAV).

PETER the family man recalled the single-minded enthusiasm of the baby for comfort and nourishment at its mother's breast, and the sheer pleasure and contentment as the milk began to flow. The illustration is apt. Desire, strong and instinctive, precedes the satisfaction, and growth follows as a divinely appointed consequence, not as a conscious human intention.

Whether we interpret 'word' as meaning the Scripture, or as meaning Christ, matters little. If we feed on the Scripture we are led to Christ and if we feed on Christ we can hardly ignore the Scripture. The crucial condition is that we have a desire, strong and insatiable, to be spiritually fed. Oh for an enhanced desire to find complete satisfaction in Christ!

> *Now none but Christ can satisfy,*
> *No other name for me;*
> *There's love and life and lasting joy,*
> *Lord Jesus, found in thee.*

> (B.E. SASB 547)

The metaphor of the baby seeking comfort and nourishment, like most metaphors has a flaw. In due course, the baby is weaned off milk on to solid foods, a point Paul made quite strongly to the Corinthians (1 Cor 3:2), but Peter did not have a weaning process in mind; to him, the milk of the word was a total food for our salvation (v.2). Having once tasted that the Lord is good (v.3) it is inconceivable that we would seek any other source of sustenance.

PRAYER
> *O Lord,*
> *Create in me a zeal*
> *To feed my soul upon the word divine.*
> *And let me know and feel,*
> *That life, abundant life, is mine. Amen.*

PRAYER
SUBJECT
> *People of influence who undermine faith.*

THE FAITHFULNESS OF JEREMIAH

READING JEREMIAH 25:1–3
'For twenty-three years – from the thirteenth year of Josiah son of Amon king of Judah until this very day – the word of the Lord has come to me and I have spoken to you again and again, but you have not listened' (v.3, NIV).

THE FAITHFULNESS of Jeremiah shines through this verse. Twenty-three years of prophesying to a people resistant to his message, speaks volumes concerning Jeremiah's tenacity and endurance. True, there were times when he wished to surrender his privileges as a prophet, but such was his conviction that he simply had   15:18; 20:7–12
to continue prophesying. Was not the word of God to him like a 'fire, shut up in my bones'? If prophecies of   20:9
judgment were an irritant to the ears of the Israelites, the same prophecies were an affliction to the prophet, but he saw himself with no alternative: he had been given a command by God and he had to obey.   1:4–10

From another angle, this same period of time represented an enormous amount of divine grace. The promise given by God to Jeremiah that he would be with him and rescue him was amply fulfilled. That grace was not   1:8
always of the most comforting kind. Jeremiah must often have squirmed on his bed of nails to find relief, but always he had available to him a dynamic contact with God. He heard the word of the Lord; knew it as the only   20:11
authoritative word for himself and the people, and   24:4–7
proceeded to be God's man in a rebellious society.

Jeremiah knew, as we all should know, that there is no viable alternative to obeying God. Whatever God requires of us, that we must do, and he helps us to find our joys in obedience.

> *Thee, only thee, resolved to obey;*   PRAYER
> *My will in all things to resign,*
> *And know no other will but thine.*
> (Charles Wesley, SASB 509)

THE FAITHFULNESS OF GOD

READING JEREMIAH 25:4–7
'And though the LORD has sent you all his servants the prophets again and again, you have not listened or paid any attention' (v.4, NIV).

IN SPITE OF THE INCONSTANCY of his people God continued to send his prophets. Throughout the long years of their history God never left himself without true witnesses in Israel. Inevitably, the prophets expressed v.3b; Isa 1:1–3 judgment, but behind the judgment there was love. Isa 14:1,2 Jeremiah's reference to the constant supply of prophets throughout their history reminds us of the parable Jesus told of the tenants of the vineyard who ill-treated the messengers the owner sent, resolving in the end, when Matt 21:33–41 the owner sent his son, to kill him. God's faithfulness was costly to him.

We would expect this tenacious, unyielding regard from God. Does not his greatness in creation, the care with which our world has been made, the varied plant and animal life, provision of food, beauty, music, language, family and friends point to an incredible and imaginative depth of caring in God? Nevertheless, while our instincts expect this of God, our minds are surprised. Surely, even God, the loving, patient God must reach a point where he calls a halt to his people's endless and wilful disobedience, declaring that a new start is required.

Reasonable though that may be, and Jeremiah stresses the fact that God's tolerance of their misdemeanours is at an end, God still holds on. There will be punishment, captivity, refining and then, a return to Jerusalem. 27:22 God's faithfulness continued and continues still.

PRAISE

Was ever faithfulness displayed
To match the faithfulness of God?
He reaches all whose feet have strayed,
Regardless of which road is trod.

SELF-INFLICTED WOUNDS

READING JEREMIAH 25:4–14
"'But you did not listen to me," declares the LORD, "and you have provoked me with what your hands have made, and you have brought harm to yourselves'" (v.7, NIV).

THE WILL OF GOD for the Israelites was simple: they would have a land flowing with milk and honey, and if they kept the covenant they would be God's 'treasured possession . . . a holy nation'. Living in the favour of God meant victory in battle, all the benefits of divine grace and an expanding quality in their fellowship with God. 'How gladly', God said through Jeremiah, 'would I treat you like sons . . . I thought you would call me "Father"'. Instead, the nation chose the paths of disobedience. Like children, responsible for their own injuries because they removed safety barriers and roamed at will in hazardous areas, their wounds were self-inflicted.

Exod 3:17

Exod 19:5,6

3:19

Over the years society has been consistently blurring the guidelines of responsible behaviour and has then proceeded to destroy as many of these safeguards as possible. In consequence, our problems and self-inflicted wounds have increased.

We are not simplistic enough today to believe that prosperity is our birthright. Furthermore, we have learned that faith is crucial, and faith grows as it is tested by stresses, hardship, disasters and suffering. Even so, God's will for us exceeds our imaginings. He desires us to be united with Christ; to function as his body on earth. It follows that those who choose against God's purpose for them will inevitably wound themselves.

1 Pet 1:7

Eph 3:20

John 15:4

Eph 4:11–13

O what peace we often forfeit,
O what needless pain we bear,
All because we do not carry
Everything to God in prayer!
(Joseph Medlicott Scriven, SASB 645)

TO PONDER

THE MOST BITTER CUP

READING JEREMIAH 25:15–38 (30–3)
"'The tumult will resound to the ends of the earth, for the LORD will bring charges against the nations; he will bring judgment on all mankind and put the wicked to the sword'" (v.31, NIV).

3:19   THE LOVE OF GOD so tenderly portrayed in Scripture, not least by Jeremiah, does not preclude the existence of judgment and its application. The other side of freedom is accountability and God, who has never left mankind in any culture without a moral sense, expects people to behave responsibly.

v.15
vv.19–26
v.18   The cup of wrath which all nations related to Israel are to drink, will be drunk first by the people in Jerusalem and the other cities of Judah. Obviously, this is a figurative, and most relevant way, of describing a powerful series of prophecies. Mankind has never been free to sin with impunity. Whether accountability for sin is acknowledged or not, the consequences of wrongdoing remain. One of the elements of wrath is the inevitability

Rom 1:18
Rom 6:23a of judgment. As surely as night follows day, judgment follows sin. 'The wages of sin is death', but not always are the consequences long delayed. With Judah, their

v.18 captivity in Babylon was about to start. As for Egypt where those who escaped Babylon fled against the

42:19 advice of Jeremiah, taking the prophet with them, their destruction by Nebuchadnezzar, king of Babylon, was

43:10–13 the subject of another prophecy.

     We can be sure that God will judge wisely, with all the love he revealed in sending Jesus as our Saviour, but we misunderstand his holiness and love if we neglect the idea of judgment.

PRAYER   *O Saviour, search my heart today*
And tell me all thou findest there!
I must more closely dwell with thee;
O grant me this, my earnest prayer!
(Miriam M. Richards, SASB 618)

THE FAITHFULNESS OF BARUCH

READING JEREMIAH 26:1–9
'The priests, the prophets and all the people heard Jeremiah speak these words in the house of the LORD' (v.7, NIV).

BARUCH WAS A FRIEND and faithful associate of Jeremiah for over twenty years. Scholars believe that most of chapters 26 to 45 come from his hand. The prophecy recorded in this chapter also appears in chapter 7, but this account in the third person is believed to be from the pen of Baruch, Jeremiah's biographer.

With a true secretary's self-effacement, Baruch keeps himself out of the reports until Jeremiah makes the purchase of some family property and requires Baruch to handle the deeds. His father and grandfather are named; his brother Seraiah is described as a staff officer for king Zedekiah; Baruch could therefore have been a person of some consequence whose contacts helped Jeremiah at certain testing times. It was Baruch who wrote down the prophecies Jeremiah desired him to declare in the temple, reading them from the room of Gemariah, son of Shaphan the secretary. Baruch had sufficient acceptance to be called upon to read the prophecies again to the officials and be given a friendly warning that he and Jeremiah should hide. 32:12 51:59 vv.16,24, cf 36:10a 36:4-81 36:10 36:11-15, 36:19

When Baruch, this stout-hearted friend of Jeremiah found the strain too much, God had a special word for him alone. In surrendering his own ambitions to serve Jeremiah, he enhanced his worth to God who rewarded him accordingly. Although there is no record of how and when Jeremiah died it appears as though Baruch escaped with his life, surviving his master by some years. God blessed Jeremiah in many ways, not least by the loyalty and service of the faithful Baruch. 45:1ff 45:5a 45:5b

Think about, and name, the friends who enable you to fulfil your tasks. Thank God for their friendship, encouragement and positive assistance. SOMETHING TO DO

A RIOT IN THE TEMPLE

READING 26:7–19 (10–16)
'But as soon as Jeremiah finished telling all the people everything the
LORD had commanded him to say, the priests, the prophets and all the
people seized him and said, "You must die!"' (v.8, NIV).

WOL 14, 15
Mar 94; 7:1–15

2 Kgs 23:29–
35

vv.4–6

THIS IS BARUCH'S ACCOUNT of the prophecy Jeremiah
made in the temple during the tumultuous days which
followed the death of Josiah, the rapid anointing and
banishment of Jehoahaz, and the crowning of Jehoia-
kim. Having gathered in the temple to hear a message of
encouragement the people were incensed by the harsh
words Jeremiah had for them.

It is significant that those who should have known
better were so prominent in creating the riot. Priests and
prophets should hold the values and share the perspec-
tives of God, they should be open to the possibility of
insights which challenge their assumptions. However,
Jeremiah had clashed with them before and knew them

5:30, 31

as participants in the downfall of the nation. Initially,
priests and prophets had combined within themselves
the concepts of worship and loyalty to God, but the more
formalised their religion became, the greater grew the
dangers of spiritual stagnation and self-seeking. God
needed a prophet like Jeremiah at this time.

vv.8, 11

v.16

Baruch's brief description heightens the threat to
Jeremiah's life, but we have a feeling of relief that the
civic authorities displayed the insight the religious
leaders lacked. How important it is that we who belong
to God should remain sensitive and open towards him.

TO PONDER

*O let me hear thee speaking
In accents clear and still,
Above the storms of passion,
The murmurs of self-will.*

(John Ernest Bode, SASB 862)

WORDS OF GRACE

READING 1 PETER 2:4–8
'You also, like living stones, are being built into a spiritual house to be a holy priesthood, offering spiritual sacrifices acceptable to God through Jesus Christ' (v.5, NIV).

IT IS INTERESTING to observe how Peter, so thoroughly nurtured in the ways of Judaism, with its emphasis on the Temple, the priesthood and the sacrificial system, moved away from those important symbols to the realities of faith.

Peter commences by referring to Christ as the living Stone (v.4). The disciples had good reason to recall our Lord's use of this metaphor following the dramatic parable of the vineyard and the tenants, when he quoted the Psalmist (Mark 12:10; Ps 118:22,23). Before the Sanhedrin, Peter, forthright as ever, made the same reference (Acts 4:11). In this letter he turns to the same authority (v.7), preceding it with the statement that we are to regard ourselves as living stones being built into a spiritual house, exercising a spiritual priesthood and offering spiritual sacrifices. It is an accurate view of the ideal Church. God's people are required to be spiritually oriented.

Peter does not proceed to define spiritual sacrifices, but it is unlikely that he differed from Paul who to the Romans wrote, 'offer your bodies as living sacrifices, holy and pleasing to God – which is your spiritual worship' (Rom 12:1). To the Philippians, Paul referred to himself as a drink offering being poured out (Phil 2:17), and he referred to their generosity as a sacrifice acceptable to God (Phil 4:18). The writer to the Hebrews refers to the offering of praise, doing good and sharing with others, as sacrifices with which God is well pleased (Heb 13:15,16). Obviously, these are the sacrifices which please God best, and which we can all make.

PRAYER
> *Take my love; my Lord, I pour*
> *At thy feet its treasure store;*
> *Take myself, and I will be*
> *Ever, only, all for thee.*
> (Frances Ridley Havergal, SASB 525)

PRAYER SUBJECT *People enslaved by drugs.*

INEQUALITY

READING JEREMIAH 26:17–24 (20–4)
'Furthermore, Ahikam son of Shaphan supported Jeremiah, and so he was not handed over to the people to be put to death' (v.24, NIV).

JEREMIAH WAS NOT ALONE in his prophetic work in Jerusalem. Even though we feel we are fighting a battle cf 1 Kgs 19:18 without allies, it is rarely so. Another prophet, Uriah son of Shemaiah, was also tuned into God, hearing and v.20 proclaiming the same message as Jeremiah, but when the king's anger was turned against him and he fled to Egypt, he was forcibly returned and ruthlessly executed. vv.21–3 So often life seems to handle people and events unevenly. It would be easy to say he lacked the kind of v.24 friends Jeremiah possessed, or, more importantly, that it was a failure in providential care.

To question providence is possible in every generation. Why did Peter and Paul die as martyrs and John live to be a very old man? In recent years, why did some Christian pastors die in prison camps while others survived to the day of liberation?

The questions point to purposes we have difficulty in perceiving. Common sense and our natural expectations stop short at those insights which are peculiar to faith, and it is faith which assures us we are in the hands of God. Peter and Paul were no less in God's care when they were martyred than when they were being miracu-Acts 12:1–19; lously freed.
16:22–36 A Christian always has the grace to do what he is required to do, and the larger plan of God will become clear when we reach our eternal home and have the eyes to see and mind to understand.

TO PONDER
I'm not outside thy providential care,
I'll trust in thee!
I'll walk by faith thy chosen cross to bear,
I'll trust in thee!

(John Lawley, SASB 761)

THE YOKE OF BONDAGE

READING JEREMIAH 27:1–15 (1–7)
'Tell this to your masters: With my great power and outstretched arm I made the earth and its people and the animals that are on it, and I give it to anyone I please' (vv.4b, 5, NIV).

AN OX'S YOKE fastened to his neck would cause any group of people to gather around Jeremiah. He had an unpalatable message for them and the surrounding nations: they were to submit to Nebuchadnezzar, the king of Babylon. We note that God calls the pagan king 'his servant', a designation repeated later and paralleled by the description of king Cyrus of Persia as God's anointed. We entertain no difficulty with God's right to dispose of the earth as he chooses, but the surprise to the Israelites, of the choice of Nebuchadnezzar, must find an echo within us because of the tyrants who have ruled with such ruthless power at certain times in history.

v.2

v.6

v.6, 43: 10

Isa 45:1

To this word of Jeremiah's we must add our Lord's comment to Pilate that he, Pilate, would have no power had God not given it; and the instructions of Paul and Peter to obey the civic authorities. Again, we have to consider a strategy of God larger than our powers of comprehension, but, clearly, God is prepared to use ungodly powers to achieve his ends.

John 19:11

Rom 13:1;

Titus 3:1; 1

1 Pet 2:13

Perhaps God is not looking for great armies to combat powerful enemies, but, rather, is looking for his people to act justly, love mercy and walk humbly with him. Are not these the people upon whom God will spread his favours?

Micah 6:8

> *O Lord,*
> *Let me but concentrate*
> *Upon my life's priorities,*
> *And in my spirit replicate*
> *Your own eternal qualities. Amen.*

PRAYER

DETERMINING THE TRUTH

READING JEREMIAH 27:16–22
'If they are prophets and have the word of the LORD, let them plead with the LORD Almighty . . .' (v.18a, NIV).

JERUSALEM, for excellent reasons, was a proud city.
2 Sam 5:6–10 Was it not virtually impregnable? Had not an astute
Hezekiah given it a water supply to enable it to with-
2 Kgs 20:20 stand an extended siege? Even so, it was still a small city
with a small city's capacity for intrigue and gossip. In
rapidly flowing concentric waves, news of central events
would spread to the outlying areas until almost everyone
would be aware of them. The conflict between Jeremiah
and the prophets of Jerusalem must, therefore, have
stimulated many wagging tongues!

Jerusalem's prophets seemed to work from a political
26:7–9 or popularity base. They knew what the people wanted to
hear and they were shrewd enough to use the language
of prophecy. Perhaps their greatest sin was that of
marginalising God in the process. The precise issue
was the removal of the Temple treasures by the Baby-
2 Kgs 25:13– lonians and their return to Jerusalem. It was under-
17 standable that the people desired to have them back,
v.16 but this would not happen for quite some time, in fact, not
v.22 until the Lord willed it.

Jeremiah, having made the hard prophecy then suggested that if the prophets wanted to know the will of God
v.18 they should start praying. His word relates to petition,
that persistent seeking after the mind of God. If they
made contact with God, they too would know his will
concerning the Temple treasures. They would also learn
very much more.

TO PONDER
Beyond thy utmost wants
His love and power can bless;
To praying souls he always grants
More than they can express.
(John Newton, SASB 560)

PROPHETIC INTEGRITY

READING JEREMIAH 28:1–11

'This is what the LORD Almighty, the God of Israel, says: 'I will break the yoke of the king of Babylon. Within two years I will bring back to this place all the articles of the LORD's house that Nebuchadnezzar king of Babylon removed from here and took to Babylon' (v.2,3, NIV).

HANANIAH merits high marks for his boldness but not for his reliability. Around Jerusalem were all the evidences anyone could need that disaster on an unparalleled scale was at hand. Within Jerusalem was all the evidence needed to make a sensitive prophet realise that God could not, and probably would not, tolerate their evil ways, and that the days of his unqualified protection were over. But Hananiah still persisted with the myth of the inviolability of Jerusalem and its people.

Not only would the Temple treasures be returned in two years but Jehoiachin and the other exiles would return, so ran his prophecy. Undoubtedly, the people wanted to hear this and desperately wanted to believe it. Their desire for this false prophecy to be true was matched by Jeremiah's own desire. There was nothing cynical about his response to Hananiah, 'Amen! . . . May the Lord fulfil the words you have prophesied by bringing the articles of the Lord's house and all the exiles back to this place from Babylon.' v.6

Jeremiah suffered too much with his people to want them to suffer more, but he knew the word of the Lord and also knew the prophetic role which was to warn of dangers and disaster. Prophets, in God's view, were not v.8 meant to be comfortable people speaking comfortable words to people who were comfortable in their sin. Truth, not deception, heals.

> *Let holy truth condemn each sham;*
> *Show what thou art, and what I am.*
>   (Arthur Sydney Booth-Clibborn, SASB 446)

TO PONDER

DISENGAGEMENT

READING JEREMIAH 28:10,11
"'This is what the LORD says: 'In the same way will I break the yoke of
Nebuchadnezzar king of Babylon off the neck of all the nations within two
years.'" At this, the prophet Jeremiah went on his way' (v.11, NIV).

v.10

THE CONFRONTATION with Jeremiah heightened dramatically as Hananiah stepped forward, took the yoke off Jeremiah's neck and broke it. Whether Jeremiah was pleased or displeased we have no way of knowing. He probably secured more publicity from Hananiah's impulsive action than if the confrontation had been conducted in a more restrained manner; but Jeremiah refrained from responding aggressively. In fact, he simply walked away.

26:7–11

Did Jeremiah withdraw from the conflict because he was defeated or because he was nonplussed by Hananiah's sudden act of aggression? Probably not. It was never his style to evade conflict. We can be sure that Jeremiah did not slink away with fear in his eyes and guilt upon his face. He never played the coward's role. Rather he would withdraw with the assurance of the divine authority on his face and in his walk. He knew God was with him and would vindicate him by events. As he had indicated to Hananiah, the prophet is proved a prophet only when his predictions come true.

v.9

Thoughtful Judaeans, their hopes stirred by the words of Hananiah would suspect that Jeremiah was speaking the truth. They might also have concluded that Hananiah had gone too far, but Jeremiah had nothing to lose, and since wisdom is shown by silence as well as speech, he said nothing.

TO PONDER

The soul which looks to God,
Who hears and trusts God's given word,
Need never know distress,
Or by un-faith or fear be stirred
For God that soul will bless.

SELF-DECEPTION

JEREMIAH 28:12–17

'Then the prophet Jeremiah said to Hananiah the prophet, "Listen, Hananiah! The LORD has not sent you, yet you have persuaded this nation to trust in lies"' (v.15, NIV).

SOME TIME ELAPSED before Jeremiah returned to Hananiah to renew this battle of the prophets. God did not give Jeremiah an immediate word with which to respond, but when it came, true to the prophetic tradition, it was comprehensive and devastating. Jeremiah's wooden yoke would be replaced by an iron yoke for the nations. Hananiah had prophesied freedom within two years, and Hananiah himself would die in the current year. If prophets are proved by the fulfilment of their prophecies, Jeremiah was dramatically and totally vindicated. _v.12 v.8 v.11 v.16_

Influencing others to do wrong is a serious business. Hananiah had assumed an authority he did not possess, presenting his wishful thinking as a revelation and was therefore accountable for his own deception and the deception of others. _vv.9,17_

The problem is topical. There are those who speak with authority on the supreme rights of the individual. On these grounds euthanasia should be legalised; abortion be on demand; sexual deviancy be tolerated to a point of encouragement; drug-taking be decriminalised, and so on. Some of our false prophets have assumed the authority to set aside the Ten Commandments and the teaching of our Lord, greatly to the detriment of others. Without doubt, God will hold them accountable.

> Lord,
>   Let me but speak your will,
>   And not my own desires.
>   Let me your plans fulfil;
>   Do all your love requires.
>   This is my soul's prevailing choice
>   To speak for you with loyal voice.

A PRAYER

WORDS OF INSIGHT

READING 1 PETER 2:9,10
'But you are a chosen people, a royal priesthood, a holy nation, a people belonging to God' (v.9a, NIV).

AFTER SOME TIME even the most revolutionary statement can appear commonplace, but with imagination we can visualise the impact of Peter's words upon his readers. How greatly encouraged they must have been. To them, people rescued from a pagan culture and brought into the light of the gospel, Peter was applying some of the choicest descriptions which belonged to Judaism. In Deuteronomy (14:2) we read, 'Out of all the peoples on the face of the earth, the Lord has chosen you to be his treasured possession.' Isaiah (43:20b, 21), on behalf of God says, '. . . to give drink to my people, my chosen, the people I formed for myself that they may proclaim my praise.' In Exodus (19:6) we read, 'you will be for me a kingdom of priests and a holy nation.' Could ever a people be more honoured? And yet, Peter seems to have had little hesitation and much conviction in describing once pagan Christians in these terms.

Adding further to the status of Christians, Peter acknowledged their original lack of standing but then affirmed that they were now the people of God (v.10). Once, they were without mercy, but now, having received mercy (Rom 9:23–6) all the special privileges and fruits of chosenness had become theirs.

This emphasis upon their distinctive place in the love of God and in his strategy for the redemption of the world, could only have been a source of strength to the people. To know that we share that remarkable status with them, gives great encouragement to us. Our lives are not inconsequential. God has chosen us and we belong to him. The cost of surrendering to life's trials and losing Christ is too high for us to contemplate.

PRAYER

> *Since I must fight if I would reign,*
> *Increase my courage, Lord!*
> *I'll bear the toil, endure the pain,*
> *Supported by thy word.*
>
> (Isaac Watts, SASB 678)

PRAYER SUBJECT   *Christians living under great pressure.*

A LETTER TO BABYLON

READING JEREMIAH 29:1–9 (4–9)
'This is what the LORD Almighty, the God of Israel, says to all those I carried into exile from Jerusalem to Babylon' (v.4, NIV).

THE FIRST GROUP of exiles were taken to Babylon in 597BC. They were the elite of the country, only the poorest and less able were left. It was, therefore, to the cream of Judah that Jeremiah wrote. They also had their prophets who were not expressing the word of God, but rather, were resonating with the desires of the people to return to Jerusalem and were prophesying wrongly. In God's view the people had important lessons to learn and these could only be learned in exile. A speedy return to Jerusalem would achieve little. It is of interest to note that Jeremiah assumed the same prophetic authority in Babylon as in Jerusalem.

2 Kgs 24:10–16

vv.8,9,15,19–21

They were to settle in the land; raise their families; become good citizens; and prosper. They were also to do that most difficult thing: they were to pray for the Babylonians, their conquerors and captors. This anticipates our Lord's command for his people to pray for their enemies.

vv.5,6

v.7

Matt 5:43–8

Above all, they were to learn that God, who is the creator, and whose love takes in the whole of creation, is as accessible and powerful outside of Jerusalem as within. Their banishment from Judaea, which was the result of their persistent sinfulness, did not mean banishment from his presence. In spite of all the evidence which seemed to suggest that God had deserted them, he was with them to answer prayer, and was still determined to prosper them and fulfil his plans for them.

v.7

vv.10,11

> *I meet my God and Father everywhere,*
> *I feel his constant love; his constant care;*
> *He comes to comfort and to answer prayer,*
> *For he is God, and he is everywhere.*

PRAISE

Thank you, Lord.

GOD STILL CARES

READING JEREMIAH 29:10–11
"'For I know the plans I have for you," declares the LORD, "plans to prosper you and not to harm you, plans to give you hope and a future'" (v.11, NIV).

v.4

WORDS OF HOPE and encouragement are never far from the lips of God. Although the Babylon captivity was his response to the people's sins (note, 'all those I carried into exile') he had not cast them off, he had plans for them once they had been through the refining experience of the exile. Such is the unchanging love of God that this word of confidence remains true today. He is always planning greater things for us. All he needs to achieve them is our loving response.

> *Don't assume that God will plan for you no more,*
> *Don't assume that there's no future to explore;*
> *For your life he'll re-design, the pattern be divine;*
> *Don't think that your repentance he'll ignore.*
> (John Gowans, SASB 44)

vv,10,11.
28:11

vv.5–7

For the exiles in Babylon, Jeremiah's word must have come with refreshing power. The best of the past, namely, life in Jerusalem and the promised land, was to be linked with God's open-ended promise of a new future. With this reassurance, they could ignore the fantasies of the false prophets, and obey God's instructions to settle themselves in Babylon in readiness for their return to Jerusalem. For ourselves, there is the renewal of confidence that God looks on us with hope. As John Gowan's song further says:

TO PONDER

> *For his love remains the same,*
> *He knows you by your name,*
> *Don't think because you've failed him he despairs;*
> *For he gives to those who ask*
> *His grace for every task,*
> *God plans for you in love for he still cares.*

THE ACCESSIBLE GOD

READING JEREMIAH 29:10–14
'"You will seek me and find me when you seek me with all your heart. I will be found by you"' (vv.13,14a, NIV).

GOD IS EAGER to hear his people's prayers. He desires to be found. God does not play the child's game of hide and seek, finding a child's pleasure in evading discovery. Neither does anyone need a special gift, a brilliantly deductive mind, or extra sensitive perceptions to discover him, desirable though such qualities might be; we only need to seek him wholeheartedly. The Psalmist rightly said that as we seek with the whole heart, God comes to us. A condition everyone can meet since it is unrelated to capacity or achievement.

Ps 119:2,10

Few Israelites could have imagined a worse situation than being exiled in a foreign land. As the élite of the population they had lost valuable homes and possessions, and had the chagrin of knowing that those allowed to remain had fought over their positions and possessions. Even so, this was a most gracious, compensating word: God was still with them.

vv.1,2

Our Lord, who fulfilled both the Law and the prophets, reinforced this prophetic word most powerfully when he said that as we ask, we will receive, as we seek, we will find and as we knock, the door will be opened to us. How diligently do we seek for God?

Matt 5:17

Matt 7:7

> I searched for thee, Lord,
> But in the starry skies, I looked in vain;
> In learnèd manuals I found not thee;
> The moon said nothing in its wax and wane;
> Dumb were the hills on thy locality.
> But, as my longing heart was opened wide
> It seemed as though a veil fell from my eyes
> And lo, I found thee standing by my side,
> My God, my life's true goal, my life's true prize.

PRAISE

REACTION

READING JEREMIAH 29:24–32
'The LORD has appointed you priest in place of Jehoiada to be in charge of the house of the Lord; you should put any madman who acts like a prophet into the stocks and neck-irons' (v.26, NIV).

vv.24,25

v.26

v.29

FREQUENTLY there are people who feel strongly enough about a subject to write letters to the appropriate authorities, and in these verses we read of Shemaiah (of whom nothing more is known), who wrote to Zephaniah the priest, and going to enormous trouble to send copies of his letter around Jerusalem. The burden of the letter was to encourage Zephaniah to do his duty and treat Jeremiah like the madman he apparently was. Unfortunately for Shemaiah, the priest thought differently about Jeremiah and showed him the letter.

v.28

The instruction given for the exiles to settle down in Babylon must have surprised many, but on examination, and quite apart from the punitive aspect of the exile, there was obviously a higher wisdom at work. Since God is the God of all creation he is at home everywhere, and there is no reason why his people should be dependent upon a special geographical location to feel at home. Said Bramwell Booth: 'Every land is my fatherland because every land is my Father's land.' It was a lesson the Israelites had to learn.

Another important lesson to learn was how to live without the temple. This was achieved by the establishment of the synagogue as a meeting place and centre of learning. The exile had significant consequences for the people of Israel, in so far as they were being refined and prepared for the future.

TO PONDER

Sometimes 'mid scenes of deepest gloom,
Sometimes where Eden's bowers bloom,
By waters still, o'er troubled sea,
Still 'tis his hand that leadeth me.
(Joseph Henry Gilmore, SASB 725)

THE BOOK OF COMFORT

READING JEREMIAH 30:1–11 (8–11)
'"I am with you and will save you," declares the LORD' (v.11a, NIV).

BECAUSE GOD'S HAND weighs so heavily on the Israelites at this time, it is inevitable that judgment should be Jeremiah's dominant theme. With the cream of the nation already in Babylon and the threatening armies of Nebuchadnezzar ready to strike again, doom filled the air. However, God had comfort for the people and he instructed Jeremiah to write the words of comfort in a book. Chapters 30/31 constitute this book of con-   vv.2,3
solation. This procedure enabled the comforting words to be read over and again during the difficult days ahead, before these special prophecies could be fulfilled.

It will be noted that God promised that even the Northern Kingdom which was taken into exile in 721 BC, and scattered throughout Assyria, would be restored   2 Kgs 17:5,6,18
although it had been virtually lost to history. How this can happen is uncertain, but nothing is too hard for God.   32:27

The fear of the people as they face God's day of judgment is powerfully portrayed. They were like strong men, pale with anguish holding themselves as women hold themselves in childbirth. God does not minimise the   vv.4–6
seriousness of that day, but he affirms that, from such a deeply troubled time, they will be saved. They are   v.7
encouraged not to fear and not to be dismayed because all their cherished hopes will be met.   v.10

Great is thy faithfulness, O God my Father,   AFFIRMATION
* There is no shadow of turning with thee;*
Thou changest not, thy compassions they fail not;
* As thou hast been thou forever wilt be.*

All I have needed thy hand hath provided;
Great is thy faithfulness, Lord, unto me!
           (Thomas Obediah Chisholm, SASB 33)

HEALING WOUNDS

READING JEREMIAH 30:12–17
'"I will restore you to health and heal your wounds," declares the LORD'
(v.17a, NIV).

v.12

FROM THE HUMAN PERSPECTIVE the wounds of Israel were incurable. They had lost vital elements of their heritage. Jerusalem was no longer inviolate; the temple had been sacked by pagan hands; the most skilful, talented and influential people had been taken into captivity; and God, their God who had been their constant patron and protector, had turned against them. Generation after generation had offended God until their punishment became inevitable, and it was God who had used their enemies to effect their punishment. A lesser

25:8,9
v.14a

problem related to the way in which their allies had not assisted them, but any aid offered would have been useless. Their wound was incurable because God had

vv.14b, 15b

inflicted it.

This special book of comfort, however, held out the hope of cure because God, and only God, could cure their chronic wound. Only he could restore them to his

vv.10–11

favour and this he was most anxious to do.

Although their wound, humanly speaking, was incurable, its cure remained largely in their own hands. God would not take them on their own terms of a rebellious, flouting of his Law. They were to listen to his messen-

26:4,5

gers, turn from their evil ways and follow his laws. Without their repentance, healing and restoration would not, could not, come. Repentance, for all its pain, distress and apparent loss of self-esteem, can prove to be a

31: 18–20

very healthy exercise.

TO PONDER

Joy of the desolate, light of the straying,
  Hope of the penitent, advocate sure;
Here speaks the Comforter, tenderly saying,
  Earth has no sorrow that Heaven cannot cure.
                                    (Thomas Moore, SASB 236)

WORDS OF ADORATION

READING 1 PETER 2:10–12
'Once you had not received mercy, but now you have received mercy'
(v.10b,NIV).

> *Thy hands created me, thy hands*
> *From sin have set me free;*
> *The mercy that hath loosed my bands*
> *Hath bound me fast to thee.*
>
> (Charles Wesley, SASB 23)

Almost every reference in Scripture to mercy links us with the mercy, or as it has been differently translated, the loving-kindness, the steadfast love, which lies at the heart of God's covenant with his people. 'Know therefore that the Lord your God is God; he is the faithful God, keeping his covenant of love to a thousand generations of those who love him and keep his commands' (Deut 7:9). It was a covenant sealed by the blood of sacrifice (Exod 24:3–8). Being Gentiles, and outside of the promises, the covenanted mercy of God, Peter's readers were not a nation, but with Christ, and the covenant sealed by his blood (Heb 9:11–15), they had received mercy and become the people of God. It is on that precise premise that we too have become God's people.

Wesley's couplet is absolutely right:

> *The mercy that hath loosed my bands*
> *Hath bound me fast to thee.*

This gift of salvation with the inheritance of all the promises God made to the children of faith, who are the true children of Abraham (Rom 4:13–17), enables us to adore the God and Father of our Lord Jesus Christ. He is so good to us!

> *To God be the glory, great things he hath done!*
> *So loved he the world that he gave us his Son;*
> *Who yielded his life an atonement for sin,*
> *And opened the life gate that all may go in.*
>
> (Fanny Crosby, SASB 22)

House-bound people.

RESTORING THE INHERITANCE

READING JEREMIAH 30:18–20
'I will restore the fortunes of Jacob's tents and have compassion on his dwellings; the city will be rebuilt on her ruins, and the palace will stand in its proper place' (v.18, NIV).

WITH THE EXTRAVAGANCE of love God continues to comfort his people. The dwelling places which had suffered because of the Babylonian invasion, the city, temple and palace which had been destroyed, would all be replaced. Everything would be as it was meant to be, albeit populated by a people who, before returning to Zion, had returned to the Lord and found healing.

v.17a

It must be remembered that Jerusalem itself and the temple, as well as the people, were precious to God. He who had filled the temple with his glory, would take no pleasure in its destruction. The population, depleted because of the deportations would quickly be restored with a renewed esteem. Their community life would be re-established. Instead of labouring under the rule of a foreign king, they would have a ruler of their own chosen from among themselves, who would have a special relationship with God.

v.17b
2 Chr 5:13,14

v.19b
v.20

v.21
v.19a

There would also be joy and thanksgiving. Across the rebuilt city and from the rebuilt temple would issue the glad sounds of a people restored in the favour of God. Always, when people are rightly related to God there is rejoicing. Even though hearts may be burdened by ill health or adverse circumstance, the notes of joy and thanksgiving can clearly be heard. He who gives joy in the morning, also gives songs at midnight.

Ps 30:5 AV
Acts 16:25

PRAYER

Come, thou Fount of every blessing,
Tune my heart to sing thy grace;
Streams of mercy, never ceasing,
Call for songs of loudest praise.
(Robert Robinson, SASB 313)

A RESTORED RELATIONSHIP

READING JEREMIAH 30:21,22
'"So you will be my people, and I will be your God"' (v.22, NIV).

GOD'S GRACIOUSNESS is demonstrated yet again by
the repetition of this covenant promise, 'You will be my
people and I will be your God.' To Jeremiah it was such a
powerful thought that it is recorded five times. We can   7:23; 11:4;
assume that in his many unrecorded prophecies,   24:7; 30:22;
speeches and conversations, he used the formula again   31:33
and yet again.

So much had happened since God told Moses that
Israel would be his treasured possession. Their history   Exod 19:5
was one of sustained rebellion and occasional repen-
tance, but God never lost sight of his plans for them: he   29:11
wanted them to be his very own people. Assessed by
human judgment, Israel was totally unworthy of the trust
God had in them, but for his own good reasons God was
anxious to maintain the covenant relationship with them.
We marvel at his patience, faithfulness and the stead-
fastness of his love.

Especially do we marvel when we realise that we too
are numbered among those whom God wants to call his
own. We think we know how unworthy the Israelites
were, but we truly know how unworthy we are! We
who are advantaged more than Israel because of
Christ's coming and the gift of the Holy Spirit, still know
the power of temptation, and the conflict of evil within the
secret places of the heart. Even so, God wishes to be our   Rom 7:18,19
God and wants us to be his people. To achieve this he
has placed enormous resources at our disposal. How   John 14:15–21
can we withhold our love from a God who loves like this?

> *The King of love my shepherd is,*   PRAISE
> *Whose goodness faileth never;*
> *I nothing lack if I am his*
> *And he is mine for ever.*
>   (Henry Williams Baker, SASB 53)

WEDNESDAY 29 MARCH

GRACE AND FAVOUR

READING JEREMIAH 31:1–4
'This is what the LORD says: "The people who survive the sword will find favour in the desert; I will come to give rest to Israel"' (v,2, NIV).

JEREMIAH'S remarkable gift of poetry is a fitting vehicle for the powerful thoughts God gave him. These prophecies of comfort echo in the heart in addition to the mind. Some translations put our key verse in the past tense, AV; NASB; making the reference to the wilderness wanderings of RAV; REB Israel obvious. Without doubt, that is a prime example of people experiencing grace in the wilderness, but the use of the present tense in our chosen translation enables us to look nearer to hand than a Middle-Eastern location some three thousand years ago.

It is a surprising and delightful fact of faith that we find favour, or grace, in our wilderness experiences. Few people volunteer for the dry, arid, inhospitable places where fellowship is in short supply, and where external resources are minimal, but having experienced the special grace or favour which comes in the midst of such times, the universal testimony seems to be they were times of grace not to be missed.

John's wilderness experience was on the island of Patmos and our Lord ensured that he found grace as the Rev 1:1–3 Book of Revelation testifies. Paul would not have chosen an extended time in prison but Jesus was with him in Eph 6:19,20 power, while across the world there are valiant souls who are living the Christ-life in many difficult places. Perhaps some of them do not even realise they are in a wilderness situation!

TO PONDER

The hosts of God encamp around
The dwellings of the just;
Deliverance he affords to all
Who on his succour trust.
(Nahum Tate & Nicholas Brady, SASB 21)

GOD'S AMAZING AFFIRMATION

READING JEREMIAH 31:1–6
'I have loved you with an everlasting love' (v.3a, NIV).

WE BOW IN AWE before a statement of this magnitude and intensity. In the midst of their troubles, when they had been banished to Babylon, God used Jeremiah to declare his love for the people. They were in the process of finding grace in the wilderness. Breathtakingly, this great declaration which was directed so unconditionally to Israel is directed in a similar manner to us. He has loved us, does love us, and will love us. 'Everlasting' means precisely that!

v.2,AV

We need time for reflection in order that this glorious truth might flow refreshingly and inspirationally through our hearts and minds. Beyond our wildest dreams, our most unreasonable longings, the truth has been stated: God loves us, and that everlastingly. The God who wishes to be our God and wants us to be his people, is a God of infinite love. We are amazed that at the centre of our bewilderingly far-flung universe beats a heart of love. An insular, scientific intelligence might have been expected to reign there, but no! God's heart is warm, compassionate and loving. Instead of being subjected to direction from a remote and relatively unconcerned being, we are exposed to a caring providence. Even more than that, in the deep recesses of the heart, God, through the Holy Spirit, is making us aware of, and receptive, to his love.

v.1

Did not Jesus come as a manifestation of the ever-lasting love? It is a love from which nothing in life or in death can separate us.

John 15:9
Rom 8:31–39

> *Loved with everlasting love,*
> *Led by grace that love to know;*
> *Spirit, breathing from above,*
> *Thou hast taught me this is so.*
> (George Wade Robinson, SASB 545)

PRAISE

AN AMAZING CONSEQUENCE

READING JEREMIAH 31:1–6
'I have drawn you with loving-kindness' (v.3b, NIV).

THE COSTLINESS OF LOVE is illustrated by the fact that it cannot compel: it can only draw. Although laws and regulations can be made and the consequences of wrongdoing be established, true love can never force the loved one into compliance. This apparent weakness in love is also its strength. When love is freely returned it is a most satisfying experience. Israel, in spite of its sinfulness, was still being drawn to God by that special *Isa 54:10* love which characterised the covenant. For good reasons, many commentators cross-reference our key verse with the revelation given of God's love through *Hos 11:1–9* Hosea where the tenderness of God's love is declared, and his sadness at their rebelliousness to him made clear. In spite of their unfaithfulness, God still continued *Hos 11:4a* to lead them with the cords of kindness and ties of love.

Our Lord's parable of the prodigal son shows that even though the father's love required him to let his son go into the far country, the knowledge of that love remained with him until, reinforced by his need, it drew *Luke 15:11–32* him back to the father's home. Was not Peter drawn by *John 21:7–17* the love of Jesus after he had denied him? Who but the Christ possessed of such love would have sought Peter *Luke 24:34* out so deliberately after the resurrection? Have we not also experienced the frustration of being separated from God, and the wistfulness of that separation? Did he not draw us to himself with the cords of love, and are we not overwhelmed with joy, and gratitude that he followed this restrained yet powerful way with us?

AFFIRMATION

I am thine, O Lord; I have heard thy voice,
And it told thy love to me;
But I long to rise in the arms of faith,
And be closer drawn to thee.

(Fanny Crosby, SASB 585)

READING JEREMIAH 31:3–9

"'There will be a day when watchmen cry out on the hills of Ephraim, 'Come, let us go up to Zion, to the LORD our God.'" (v.6, NIV)

THE REMARKABLE PROMISE to rebuild the entire nation is repeated. Not only to the exiles in Babylon, who constituted a compact and definite group maintaining their national identity, with their synagogues and new forms of worship, but also to the long-since deported Northern Kingdom, this message of restoration was given. It will be remembered that this kingdom consisted of the ten tribes which, under Jeroboam, parted from king Rehoboam the son of Solomon, shortly after Solomon's death. To ensure independence from Jerusalem, Jeroboam built alternative shrines at Bethel and Dan. The Northern Kingdom was frequently known as Israel and Ephraim, thereby further adding to our confusion. *WoL 24 Mar 95* *1 Kgs 12:1ff.*

The Northern Kingdom, Ephraim, was conquered by the Assyrians and its people's deportation was virtually total. Unlike Judah, the Southern Kingdom, they were widely scattered, their land being resettled with other conquered groups by the Assyrians *2 Kgs 17:1–6* *2 Kgs 17:24–26*

Jeremiah included this widely scattered and almost lost people in this great promise. They too, being loved, would also be drawn back to God and restored. They would be given back their purity, celebrating their renewed status with timbrel and dance. The hills would become vineyards but so much more importantly, they would desire to worship in Zion again. *vv.3,4* *vv.5,6*

We all, in perfect love renewed,
Shall know the greatness of thy power,
Stand in the temple of our God
As pillars, and go out no more.
(Augustus Gottlieb Spangenberg, trs John Wesley, SASB 533) *AFFIRMATION*

SUNDAY 2 APRIL
WORDS OF GRACE

READING 1 PETER 2:11–12
'Live such good lives among the pagans that, though they accuse you of doing wrong, they may see your good deeds and glorify God on the day he visits us' (v.12, NIV).

THREE EXCELLENT REASONS are given to help us with our daily conduct. We are to remember that we are aliens and strangers in this world (1:1,17; 2:11). This world is not our permanent home: we are a pilgrim people who have to pass this way to reach our eternal dwelling place (Heb 11:13–16). Our Lord expects us to apply the norms of our true home to our pilgrim journey, regardless of our location. The parallel can be drawn with the Israelites who, as sojourners, established and were expected to maintain their special identity and codes of behaviour whether in the desert, Bashan, or Moab. We have to remember what we are and to whom we belong. God expects it of us.

Neither do we have to sin (Rom 6:14). The evil desires which master people do not have to master us, because we have been born again of imperishable seed (1:23). We have the power to abstain from sin. Peter's words carry the assumption that goodness is the natural fruit of a redeemed life (cf Matt 7:15–18) as evil is the natural fruit of the unredeemed life.

Faith can be misconstrued and some kind of censure follow. The Christian faith in Peter's day was greatly misunderstood by many. Lurid rumours, some mistakenly based on the words of Jesus, 'Take and eat; this is my body', and, 'Drink . . . This is my blood of the covenant' (Matt 26:26–8), began to circulate. However, Peter knew that our good deeds are to commend, not only us, but also the gospel we preach, in order to bring glory to God. Goodness is required of us; it is personally rewarding; it helps to achieve God's ends and, by God's great mercy, is attainable.

PRAYER

A charge to keep I have,
A God to glorify,
A never-dying soul to save,
And fit it for the sky.

(Charles Wesley, SASB 472)

PRAYER SUBJECT *For good works and strong faith in Christians.*

PAUL'S WELCOME IN JERUSALEM

READING ACTS 21:17–20a
'The next day Paul and the rest of us went to see James, and all the elders were present' (v.18, NIV).

PAUL'S LONG JOURNEY to Jerusalem had come to an end. Behind was a glorious trail of church planting and building; ahead stretched a road of hardship, albeit of confidence, because Paul was sure the Spirit was leading him. *WoL* 2–17 / Dec 94 / 20:22–24

Without delay Paul and his companions met the established leaders of the church in Jerusalem; it was important they should be given a report of the progress of the gospel in the Gentile world. We can imagine the enthusiasm of Paul as he told James and the elders how the gospel spread from Asia Minor into Europe, of his time in Athens, Corinth and Ephesus before returning to Jerusalem. Paul would also wish to hand over the money the new churches had given for the Jerusalem Christians. v.19 / 16:6ff / 17:16–34, / 18:1–18, 19:1ff / 24:17; 1 Cor 16:1–4

There must have been much joy on the part of James and the elders as they listened to this report. We are told that when they heard it, they praised God, but, surely, they did more than that! The account was stirring enough for Luke to have reported an excited celebration of faith, instead he moved immediately into a problem which was of great concern to the Jerusalem leaders. If, however, Luke's low-key report accurately reflects the situation, James and the elders had missed an occasion for celebration, even though they had a serious problem on their hands. We ought to take every opportunity we can to celebrate the work of the Holy Spirit. v.20a / v.20b

We praise you Lord for every ransomed soul;
For every power released to your control;
For every wounded heart by grace made whole;
Now loose our tongues, our feelings liberate,
And all your mercies let us celebrate. PRAISE

ALL THINGS TO ALL MEN

READING ACTS 21:20–6
"'You see, brother, how many thousands of Jews have believed, and all of them are zealous for the law'" (v.20b, NIV).

PAUL MUST HAVE BEEN GLAD that Jews in their thousands had accepted Christ as Messiah and Lord, even though some of them held rigid opinions. No doubt many of them, or their families, were known to him. However, they had heard that he was telling Christian Jews to turn away from Jewish customs and this disturbed them. Without too much difficulty they accepted that Gentiles did not need to embrace Judaism, but because Moses and the law were part of God's gift to them, they felt that Jews, having accepted Christ as Messiah, should remain as Jews. To reassure the Jewish Christians, James asked Paul to take part in a Jewish ceremony.

Given time for reflection, Paul might well have declined the offer. Harmless enough in itself, the exercise has caused many to feel that it was not like Paul to do something which could be interpreted as reinforcing the Law, and he was the apostle of freedom from the Law's requirements.

Perhaps the wisest judgment to make is that it shows Paul's eagerness to be all things to all men, in the hope that by these means he might win some. If, by taking part in this vow, some think a Nazarite vow, Paul could help his fellow Jews, it would seem a small price to pay.

Side references: 15:5, v.21, v.25, vv.22–24, Rom 8:1–4, 1 Cor 9:22, cf Num 6:1–21

TO PONDER

If I would influence my friend,
My brother's keeper try to be,
Must I not try to comprehend,
And his perspective try to see?
Then, if without committing sin
I share my friend's most common ground,
Am I not well-placed to begin
To show him how Christ's way is found?

READING ACTS 21:27–36
'Some Jews from the province of Asia saw Paul at the temple. They stirred up the whole crowd and seized him' (v.27b, NIV).

PAUL SEEMED TO ATTRACT TROUBLE as a flame attracts a moth. Almost wherever he went there was conflict, from his conversion days in Damascus, to this riot in Jerusalem which was the beginning of his journey to Rome, and subsequent martyrdom. Luke described the riot with dramatic power, giving it the authenticity of an eye-witness account. Observed by some Asian Jews who believed he had profaned the temple by taking a Gentile past the outer court which was open to anyone, they only had to cry, 'Men of Israel, help us!', and the cry would be taken up securing an immediate response. Nationalism and religious fervour combined to ensure that Paul would be beaten to death. Fortunately, the Roman guard observing the temple area from the adjacent Fortress of Antonia sounded the alarm, and Paul was rescued.

Tradition says that Paul was small of stature and not particularly robust, but he had courage enough for any situation. Although he was ready to face any conflict in his service for Christ, he was a man of extreme tenderness and, other than Christ, none knew the nature of love better than he.

Christ himself, the Prince of Peace, divided people because his gospel threatened their assumptions, complacency and security. Perhaps it is almost inevitable that a gospel of love will evoke opposition, even hate at times, in some people.

9:19–25

v.29 , v.28

v.30

vv.31–36

2 Cor 10:10

cf v.39, with
19:29–31,
2 Cor 11:29,
1 Cor 13:1ff

Souls shall be saved from the burden of sin,
Doubt shall not darken his witness within,
Hell hath no terrors, and death hath no sting;
Love is victorious when Jesus is King.
(Charles Silvester Horne, SASB 166)

TO PONDER

THURSDAY 6 APRIL
ASSUMPTIONS

READING ACTS 21:27–9,37–22:1
"'Aren't you the Egyptian who started a revolt and led four thousand terrorists out into the desert some time ago?'" (v.38, NIV)

v.29	THE RIOT WAS CAUSED by an assumption. Some Asian Jews had seen the Ephesian Trophimus in the city with Paul and had assumed that Paul had taken him into the temple area, an act which, if true, would have been both illegal and profane. It was, however, merely an assumption. Paul's presence in the temple area followed the assumption by some Jewish Christians that Paul was actively campaigning against Jewish traditions. Be-
v.21	cause they had accepted Jesus as the Messiah, who was the logical and revealed fulfilment of Jewish Law and messianic expectation, they assumed that the Jew-
v.20b	ish culture should be maintained, even though special conditions had been formulated for Gentile Christians.
v.25	James and the elders also made the assumption that if Paul engaged in this purification ritual, everything would
vv.22–24	be nicely smoothed over.

When he and his troops rescued Paul, the commander assumed that he was rescuing an Egyptian terrorist from

v.38

being lynched. He was surprised when he learned that this beaten, unkempt yet articulate man was both Jew

v.39; 22:27

and Roman. What a story he had to tell in the officers' mess that night!

We ourselves frequently think and act from inadequately formed assumptions. It is so easy to comment on people and situations in a judgmental way, without pausing to consider that there may be facts which if known would modify our comments. Because of his love and wisdom it is comforting that, ultimately, judgment is in the hands of the Lord.

John 5:22

PRAYER

O Lord, grant me your charity
And blend my judgments with your love.
I need your love to see with clarity
The motives which make others move.

A GREAT COMMUNICATOR

READING ACTS 22:1–13
'When they heard him speak to them in Aramaic, they became very quiet' (v.2, NIV).

COURAGE PAUL HAD in abundant measure. His bruises and dishevelled appearance only seemed to make him more determined to carry the contest back to his opponents. Their violence had given him a platform and the opportunity was too good to miss! We take note of his powers of communication. To the commander of the guard he spoke in Greek, the language he knew. When he addressed his fellow Jews, he obviously spoke in Aramaic, the common language of the people, but quite as importantly, he spoke to the heart as well as the mind.

v.39

We observe how Paul captured, and held, their attention. He told them he was a Jew born in one of the chief cities of Asia where there was a strong Jewish community, with parents sufficiently wealthy, we presume, for him to be brought up in Jerusalem. As though that was not enough, had he not been taught by the famous Gamaliel, becoming extremely zealous for the law? Adding further to his credibility, he outlined his persecution of the Christians, indicating that this was done not on his own initiative, but with the knowledge and full authority of the high priest and council.

v.3

vv.4,5

Comparing this with the earlier account given of Paul's conversion, we see that here Paul stressed, without compromising the truth, the status of Ananias in the Jewish community. The crowd must have been captivated by his eloquence and credentials. Paul spoke as one who stood where they were standing.

9:1–19; WoL
19–27 Feb 93
v.12

> *Must I not try to stand beside*
> *That one whom Christ wants me to guide*
> *To faith, and faith's great confidence*
> *In God, and in his providence?*

TO PONDER

CHOSEN AS A WITNESS

READING ACTS 22:6–16

'The God of our fathers has chosen you to know his will and to see the Righteous One and to hear words from his mouth' (v.14, NIV).

vv.6–12

IT WAS REMARKABLE that the crowd continued to listen spellbound as Paul spoke of his encounter with Jesus, his blindness, journey into Damascus, and the visit of Ananias that devout and highly respected Jew. The ministry of Ananias was validated by the restoration of sight to Paul, but again, there was no adverse response by the crowd as Paul recalled the words of Ananias, 'The

v.14a.

God of our fathers has chosen you . . .'. Paul was recounting the truth, of course, but he was also emphasising the continuity of God's work in and through Judaism. He could discern no real conflict with the past, only its fulfilment in Christ.

v.14b

Ananias also told him that he would see and hear Jesus, a meeting which took place in the very temple he was accused of profaning, but the Lord's words were of

vv.17,18

warning because of the disbelief of the Jews. Still the crowd listened intently, as Paul went on to reveal that he believed the Jews would accept his credibility because of his persecution of the Christians, and his part in the

vv.19,20

martyrdom of Stephen. However, Jesus knew more than Paul, indicating that he would be sent far away from

v.21

Jerusalem.

Paul seemed almost to believe still, that his testimony was enough to give him acceptance, but when he spoke of his mission to the Gentiles the crowd's anger broke

v.22

out again. Barriers of élitism and dogma are not that easily broken down.

AFFIRMATION

I'll go in the strength of the Lord,
In paths he has marked for my feet;
I'll follow the light of his word,
Nor shrink from the dangers I meet.

(Edward Turney, SASB 734)

TRUTH AND TRIUMPH

READING LUKE 19:28—44.

"'If you had known, even you, especially in this your day, the things that make for your peace! But now they are hidden from your eyes'" (v. 42, NKJV).

ONE OF THE GREAT MISTAKES of that first Palm Sunday was that truth and triumph were not linked by those who required them most, sinners in need of salvation. The people shouting and singing proclaimed triumph, but it was their idea of triumph which they desired. Unfortunately it was a triumph without truth. Their ideas of a kingdom of wealth and power were self-centred and, as such, very different from the righteousness, the holiness God desired. The essence of sin is self, and whenever self is primary, truth is absent.

When self is crucified, truth and triumph come together in the great dynamic of salvation. Power to grow in Christ reaches holy proportions, and power to witness approaches first-century standards. May our hosannas ring with truth today, declaring the triumph of Christ in our hearts! May we affirm the King who comes in the name of the Lord, as the ruler of the Kingdom of God in us! May our singing and praising be offered on his terms of righteousness. This is the truth of a genuine love for the Master. This truth alone brings genuine triumph, and not the tragic judgment of that first Palm Sunday.

Then will Christ rejoice over us because we have grasped the truth of his triumph over evil. We have experienced its application in our lives, freeing us from sin and for himself; for the inheritance that is ours as heirs of the King (Gal 4:6, 7).

> *Triumph without truth is a sham.*
> *Truth without triumph is a tragedy.*
> *Truth wedded to triumph is GLORY!*

PRAYER   *Lord, grant me the openness of heart to receive your truth, and to share the joy of your triumph over all the forces of evil. Amen.*

PRAYER SUBJECT   *For a spirit of joy among God's people.*

A LAST CHANGE

READING MARK 11:12–19
'Then He taught, saying to them, "Is it not written, 'My house shall be called a house of prayer for all nations'? But you have made it a 'den of thieves.'"' (v.17, NKJV).

> *SELF IS square on the throne,*
> *And the only concern is its own.*
> *Though the Saviour may come,*
> *He's not the Chosen One,*
> *For self is square on the throne.*

v.17

Eph 3:16

Luke 19:47

The Saviour of the world, his heart hungry for the souls of men, comes to his own, but their gaze is no longer upward to their God. It is downward to the things of this world. Because of this, God's house becomes a market place in which to hawk one's wares; a 'den of thieves'. Living during the most glorious visitation in the whole of salvation history, they reject 'the riches of his glory'. Luke writes, 'the chief priests, the scribes, and the leaders of the people sought to destroy him'.

Self upon the throne of life can only see the world of things and try to exploit them for personal gain. And when the light of truth crosses its path it often reacts with rejection and violent hostility.

John 15:12

Since that day when Jesus taught in the temple, the heritage of salvation history has been enriched by some two thousand years of continued involvement with man. These two thousand years plead with us to yield to our best desires for purity of heart, and to our Lord's command that we should love as he has loved.

TO PONDER

> *Turn your eyes upon Jesus,*
> *Look full in his wonderful face,*
> *And the things of earth will grow strangely dim,*
> *In the light of his glory and grace.*

HAVE FAITH

READING MARK 11:20–4
'So Jesus answered and said to them, "Have faith in God"' (v.22, NKJV).

IN THE MORNING on the way to Jerusalem, Jesus and the disciples came upon the fig tree he cursed the day before, which had now withered. It is fitting that this day should begin with a display of Christ's authority, for it will be spent debating with Jewish leaders. Jesus is not merely trying to establish his authority. He is proclaiming it, and basing his teachings on that authority.

11:27–33

We can accept Christ or reject him. However, we cannot decide the outcome of these choices. Acceptance brings blessing; rejection, condemnation. This is a divine absolute. Man has only one option if he is to be blessed of God, and Christ clearly establishes that option as his followers exclaim: 'Rabbi, look! The fig tree which you cursed has withered away.' Jesus responds, 'Have faith in God.' At the very beginning of this day, Christ provides the answer to every dilemma, every problem, every concern, every difficulty, every question that will ever face any person, 'Have faith in God'.

v.22

In today's passage we are confronted by a people who stand at the very centre of a life-changing event. They are caught up to a greater or lesser degree in a major issue of the day, namely, has the Saviour, the Anointed One of God, come in the person of this carpenter's son from Nazareth? Could this be the day of their divine visitation? Could it be ours?

Jesus says, 'Yes, "Have faith in God."' Trust the promises embodied in his only Son. Follow him, walk with him, talk with him, become his very own.

'Watch therefore . . . lest coming suddenly, he find you sleeping. And what I say to you, I say to all: "Watch!"' (Mark 13:35–37).

TO PONDER

THE PLOT CONTINUES

READING MARK 14:1–11.

'. . . the chief priests and the scribes sought how they might take him by trickery and put him to death' (v.1, NKJV).

vv.3–9

WHILE WE ARE NOT CERTAIN that the anointing of Jesus actually takes place at this time, it is a preparation for his impending death. The plot to take Jesus' life continues to unfold as Mark informs us of Judas' infamous meeting with the chief priests. Approached by Judas, the chief priests make one of the most tragic statements ever recorded: 'And when they heard it, they were glad, and promised to give him money.' Of Judas, Matthew says, 'It would have been good for that man if he had not been born.'

vv.10–11

v.11

26:24.

The crucifixion is a trans-historical event. Every sin of humanity was at work to nail Christ to the cross. And this tragedy goes on today. The writer to the Hebrews says of those who fall away from the light, 'they crucify again for themselves the Son of God, and put him to an open shame.' And again: 'Of how much worse punishment, do you suppose, will he be thought worthy who has trampled the Son of God underfoot, counted the blood of the covenant by which he was sanctified a common thing, and insulted the Spirit of grace?'

Heb 6:6

Heb 10:29

During Holy Week we are reminded of a world gone mad; lost in the fog of its folly and self-indulgence, wasting its capacity for worship on false gods, while Christ, the only redeemer, continues to wage war 'against principalities, against powers, against the rulers of the darkness of this age'. In an ultimate sense, the battle has already been won, but in the present sense, the battle still rages.

Eph 6:12

John 16:33

SOMETHING
TO DO

Allow our hearts to be moved by the sin of the world, as Christ was moved. Plead in prayer for a spirit of forgiveness and reconciliation to prevail, and pray for a mighty movement of God's Spirit in our land.

PREPARATION FOR POWER

READING MATTHEW 26:36–46.
'"Watch and pray, lest you enter into temptation. The spirit indeed is willing, but the flesh is weak'" (v.41, NKJV).

THE TRAGEDY OF HOLY WEEK is about to break loose in a flood of events. Jesus revealed his betrayer, finished the Passover meal, prophesied the scattering of the flock, and specifically, the denial of Peter. Now, Jesus takes Peter, James, and John with him into the grove of olive trees to pray.

v.25
v.30
v.31, v.34
v.37

The weight of the moment centres upon the very spirit of Christ in that garden. He prays for mercy: 'let this cup pass'; yet affirms his willingness to accept his Father's plan no matter what may come: 'nevertheless, not as I will, but as you will'. Here is a graphic commentary on spiritual power.

v.39

Where does spiritual power come from? Is it like some kind of divine lightning, or energy force? Hardly. Spiritual power is more natural than that. It is a product of association, directly proportional to the intimacy of our relationship with God. No amount of Bible study, nor the worship of a lifetime, can replace prayer in developing a personal, intimate walk with God which is the only preparation for spiritual power.

Let us make this Holy Week a covenanting event with respect to prayer, determining, or reaffirming, to make prayer a consistent spiritual discipline. For the spirit is still willing, and the flesh is weak. We need it, and the world needs it.

v.41

Dear Lord, forgive us for taking your indwelling presence for granted. Thank you for loving us, watching over us, making us partners in your plans for the world. Help us to begin a new chapter in our devotional life as we covenant to pray more effectively because of a deeper relationship with you. Amen.

PRAYER

INTO THE ABYSS

READING JOHN 18:3–19:42.
'"Everyone who is of the truth hears my voice." Pilate said to him, "What is truth?"' (vv.37b, 38a, NKJV)

BETWEEN THE ARREST of Jesus and his crucifixion, we encounter humanity, fully clothed in its garments of sin. Pilate asks, 'What is truth?' It is not known by this sceptic from Rome. For him life is cheap, position and power worth any price, with ambition the key to any meaning. Standing face-to-face with the man whose mind held the answers to the mysteries of the universe, whose hands held the healing power for any ailment, whose very life could guarantee eternal and abundant life, Pilate steps back into the darkness of his own scepticism, down into the abyss of guilt and shame.

Matt 15:14

Matt 12:24

For the religious leaders of the day, blind leaders of the blind, truth no longer stands above them, exercising authority over them. They define darkness as truth, and, with Pilate, also step back into the abyss.

When man looks for truth within himself, he will only find darkness. Truth ever stands outside and above man, calling him to account, pointing out the direction, setting the standards.

Will it be down into the abyss or up into the light? Will we acknowledge doctrine not only in word, but also in deed, transforming it into truth? Will we deny the Saviour or profess him? Will we surrender to him or place ourselves on the throne of our lives? Good Friday poses these questions. Now is the time to answer them, by looking up into the light, by walking in the light, and

1 John 1:7

John 8:12

having fellowship with the light, the light of the world who is Jesus Christ.

AFFIRMATION

Love so amazing, so divine,
Demands my soul, my life, my all.
(Isaac Watts, SASB 136)

CONCEALING THE OBVIOUS

READING MATTHEW 27:62–66.
'. . . command that the tomb be made secure until the third day . . .' (v.64a, NKJV).

WHILE SOME RELIGIOUS LEADERS did not believe in Christ, there was a fact they could not dismiss. Though corrupt, and as faithless as their Roman rulers, they could not ignore the fact of the empty tomb. An empty tomb would witness to the Messiah and fuel the flames of hope among a people desperately in search of a Saviour. So they tried to keep Christ in the tomb!

Today, followers of darkness labour no less passionately, no less subtly and craftily, to stop the proclamation of salvation through the shed blood of the man on the cross. In spite of all of the evidence of his life, death, and resurrection, people still dispute, and malign, all to keep Christ in the tomb. Satan labours unceasingly to keep the stone over the door, for if Christ is not risen then our faith is vain, and lost humanity is imprisoned within that tomb with Christ.

1 Cor 15:14

However, the effort is as futile today as it was long ago. Nothing could, or can, keep the risen Christ out of his world. Jesus holds the power of life and death, both spiritual and physical, in his hands. He will be the Saviour, no matter what unbelief does or says. He is the King of Glory.

In league with the Holy Spirit, may our lives proclaim with great persuasion that the closed tomb is an illusion, implying power where there is no power. If we believe the word of Jesus; that death cannot hold the anointed one of God, then Christ and his eternal and abundant life will ours. The tomb was not the end, but a glorious beginning!

Matt 16:21

> *Death cannot keep his prey,*
> *Jesus, my Saviour.*
> (Robert Lowry, SASB 148)

PRAISE

EASTER SUNDAY 16 APRIL
A NEW AND POWERFUL HOPE

READING MATTHEW 28:1–8
'He is not here; for he is risen, as he said' (v.6a, NKJV).

> *THE CROSS speaks for the futility of man's effort,*
> *Easter for the fulfilment of man's hope.*
> *The cross stands as the handiwork of man,*
> *Easter as the handiwork of God.*
> *Any man can build a cross,*
> *Only God can produce an Easter.*
>
> (Will Sessions, 'Week of the Cross', p. 89)

Can it be true? Has he risen indeed? It is clear from the scriptural accounts of that first Easter morning, that hope in a living Christ had died with the crucifixion of Jesus (Luke 24:1). In spite of an empty tomb, and heavenly messengers proclaiming the resurrection, Matthew reports 'some doubted' (Matt 28:17). Of Mary's account Mark says, 'they did not believe' (16:11). In response to the witness of the Emmaus travellers Mark writes: 'they did not believe them either' (16:13).

After the anguish of Friday, the Easter story seemed too good to be accepted on the word of a few people. In response to this doubt, and to doubt ever after, Luke reports that Jesus 'presented himself alive after his suffering by many infallible proofs, being seen by them forty days and speaking of the things pertaining to the kingdom of God' (Acts 1:3). Dramatically, the hope of the followers again began to stir.

Even so, the new hope did not come easily, but come it did. And this new hope in Christ has ever stood as a testimony to the power of the gospel to accomplish all of the good that it has promised, throughout the whole of Christian history. It is on the basis of this new hope that Paul describes the gospel as 'the power of God to salvation for everyone who believes' (Rom 1:16).

PRAYER: *Grant us to know in our hearts, as well as our minds that Jesus is alive – alive for evermore! Amen.*

PRAYER SUBJECT: *That we make every day an Easter day.*

CONNECTING WITH CHRIST

READING LUKE 24:13–35 (28–35)
'Did not our heart burn within us while he talked with us on the road, and while he opened the Scriptures to us?' (v. 32 NKJV)

IN THINKING OF EMMAUS, we picture two disciples, sad and disillusioned. Across their loftiest dreams is written the word 'failure'. With hope gone, were they not heading back to the old life, the old friendships, the old ruts? If there is anything redeeming about this event, it is that in the midst of this tragedy they talked together of all these things which had happened. While the testimonies of those early visitors to the tomb did not convince these two travellers that Jesus had risen from the grave, on that road to Emmaus they thought about those events and their meaning. As they thought and talked 'Jesus himself drew near and went with them.' Unknowingly these despondent disciples had kept a channel of communication open between themselves and God.

v.13

v.14

v.15

Someone has said, 'The winds of God are always blowing, but we must hoist the sails.' It is up to us to keep the lines of communication open between ourselves and God. Even when times are difficult, if we keep our thoughts on the Kingdom, we can always be in touch with Christ. All is never lost if our minds and hearts are open to him.

And this truth applies not only to us but to others whom we know. As we live in the Spirit, we will help another make that vital contact. Someone else will find encouragement in spirit as Christ draws near to them and ministers to their need.

O Lord Jesus, speak to us that your truth might burn within us, rekindling the flame of zeal for the things of God. We are your people. Fill us with your fullness. It is in Jerusalem, our Jerusalem, that we wish to stand, right in the centre of your will, fully indwelt by your Spirit. Amen.

PRAYER

GOD'S OMNIPOTENCE

READING LUKE 24:36–45.
'He said to them, "Why are you troubled? And why do doubts arise in your hearts?"' (v.38, NKJV)

Matt 19:26

THIS KEY VERSE could be paraphrased, 'Why this surprise and doubt? With God all things are possible. A man can rise from the dead.' The old chorus says, 'Only believe, all things are possible, only believe.' So often when we think about the omnipotence of God, we think of how it could be put to good use in our own lives, to meet our own needs, even our own wants. However, prayers centring upon ourselves often seem to carry little power.

The disciples were used to perceiving Christ in relation to their own concerns and not in terms of God's plan for them, in and through Christ. The truth that all things are possible with God has primary emphasis on what God has done, and has yet promised to do. Luke tells us that Jesus had to draw the attention of the disciples to the great prophecies of Scripture, that they might under-

vv.44,45

stand the almighty power of God in terms of his priorities, his passions and his promises.

Like the disciples, we too are prone to a narrow view of eternal truths and events, relating them largely to ourselves. As a result, we often, quite innocently but foolishly, attempt to take our destiny into our own hands. Instead of trusting God who is all-powerful, as well as all-knowing, and whose utter faithfulness calls us to leave our affairs with him, we coach him on how he might fulfil his will for our lives. It doesn't really make much sense!

PRAYER

Almighty God, how great are the things you have accomplished. Let us not make fools of ourselves by even suggesting how you might act as our God. Rather, help us to understand how great and wonderful you are and to rest our lives in your hands. Amen.

THE ESSENCE OF SAVING FAITH

READING JOHN 20:24–31.
'Blessed are those who have not seen and yet have believed' (v.29, NKJV).

JOHN ALONE RECORDS the account of Thomas, re- ferred to as the 'doubter'. But Thomas is not alone in doubting. Many of us are like him. We want to see for ourselves. We are not entirely satisfied with another person's account of an important event. Others might be duped but we would not be fooled. Doubting is not to be excused. Our chosen Scripture makes this abundantly clear. However, honest doubting is understandable. Our Lord had so much patience, he must have taught his followers over and over again, to change doubt into faith.
cf v.25
v.27b

What is the essence of this saving faith? It is not blind trust in whatever we are told, certainly not when it comes to our salvation. It is to believe the witness of those whose testimony corresponds with the truth of Scripture. Jesus often confronted the doubts of his followers with the truth of Scripture, frequently quoting the prophets.
Luke 24:44

Becoming students of God's word is not for preachers and teachers alone. It is for all of us who would bear the name of Christ as his followers. Weak faith results from lack of biblical knowledge, or uncertainty about the whole of salvation history in which the scriptural word is embedded. Strong faith comes from a growing know- ledge of the word of God, and a willingness to accept the testimony of the great cloud of witnesses, whose lives give credibility to that word. The word and the people of the word nurture those in search of truth.

> *A glory gilds the sacred page,*
> *Majestic, like the sun;*
> *It gives a light to every age;*
> *It gives, but borrows none.*
> (William Cowper, SASB 657)

AFFIRMATION

A WORLD IN THE BALANCE

READING JOHN 21:1–14
'And he said to them, "Cast the net on the right side of the boat, and you will find some." So they cast, and now they were not able to draw it in because of the multitude of fish' (v.6, NKJV).

20:22

20:23

THE PASSION OVER, we learn from John that the Holy Spirit has been given to the disciples. No doubt, as in the past for a special purpose, perhaps to keep them until the pentecostal outpouring of the Spirit. In this time of preparation, they receive a hint of their mission, but it is only a hint. We believe we know that because we find them back in the old neighbourhood where they had decided to go fishing. It is awesome, and not a little frightening, to think that the world hung in the balance, as those few men sat in a little boat on the Sea of Galilee, fishing.

After two thousand years of history the world still hangs in the balance. The fight for the souls of men and women, boys and girls, is fought in every generation and in every part of the world. But in every generation some followers of Jesus still occupy themselves by going out to fish, to satisfy their own desires rather than living to win the lost.

Oh, the Lord is calling, of that there is no doubt. But not all of the fishermen are as perceptive as those first disciples on the Sea of Galilee. They don't look at the One who is calling, as John looked at him, or they too would recognise the Master hailing them, calling them to a mission field, near or far. And the world hangs in the balance.

TO PONDER *The Lord is calling all of his followers to be witnesses to his resurrection glory. Each generation has to be challenged and won for him. Whatever ministry he has given us must be exercised in order that his Kingdom might come. Our God-given task is absolutely crucial.*

RESTORATION IS ONLY A BEGINNING

READING JOHN 21:15–23.
'And when he [Jesus] had spoken this, he said to him [Peter], "Follow me"'
(v.19, NKJV).

WHILE ALL THE GOSPELS record Peter's denial of the Lord, John alone records Peter's restoration. John reports that Christ asks Peter three times, 'do you love me?' Why ask Peter three times? Wasn't Peter sure of his love for the Master? Although nothing is more apparent from the scriptural record, than the fact that Peter loved Jesus.

vv.15–17

But perhaps Peter didn't understand what loving Jesus really meant. Jesus said, 'Simon . . . do you love me more than these?' Jesus had just finished feeding the disciples. 'Do you love me more than the others?' Or, perhaps, 'Do you love me more than the ordinary things of life?' Or, 'Do you realise that there is something special about loving me? When I'm gone from your sight again, are you going back to the old way, which is not the way at all? Instead of feeding my lambs will you again go back fishing? Because, if you really love me, Peter, it's going to cost you your very life. Do you love me more than this very life you possess?'

v.15

vv.18,19

Love is the final and ultimate ingredient in the mix of disciple preparation. As the light begins to dawn on a new day of promise, this special ingredient is held up, and we begin to understand that only love with integrity, perseverance, humility and compassion, can fit us to break the bonds of time and space to fulfil our divine calling in Christ. It is so easy to say, 'I love you Jesus.' But love needs to be nurtured through his word, faithful service, and the intimate discipline of prayer to make it strong and sure.

Let love be first, let love be last,
Its light o'er all my life be cast.
(Thomas C. Marshall, SASB 620)

TO PONDER

COMMISSIONED TO RELATIONSHIP

READING MATTHEW 28:16–20

'"Go therefore and make disciples of all the nations . . . and lo, I am with you always, even to the end of the age' (vv. 19a,20b, NKJV)

MATTHEW RECORDS the Great Commission as Christ's last message. Was it to be a message of comfort and encouragement, seeking to strengthen his followers for his departure? No! Rather it was a message centring on duty and obligation. The disciples were exhorted to 'Go' and proclaim the gospel.

The question arises, however, are comfort and encouragement necessarily divorced from duty and obligation? Not when it comes to following the will of God to 'go . . . and make disciples of all the nations.' When the Great Commission becomes our personal commission, it is not so much a sending out by a lord of the manor to do his bidding, as an invitation to join the Lord in the work in which he himself is engaged.

The Great Commission calls us not to labour for the Master as much as to share fellowship with him. This is emphasised in his closing words, 'Lo, I am with you always.' There is a vital difference between working for, and working with, the Lord. To work with the Lord is to

John 15:14,15. highlight relationship. In so doing, devotion and communication take on primary importance. There is no less work to do, but far less bondage in obligation, drudgery and

cf Mark 16:20 routine. Duty and obligation can become very legalistic, but when seen in terms of an intimate relationship, they

John 14:15 take on the nature of love. Love to God is always expressed in the obedience of a free and committed will to him.

PRAYER *Dear Lord, we would know you, and how better can we come to know you than by working with you in this great harvest of souls? May we hear you speak, feel your love, understand the passion of your heart, be fruitful in your service, and may our hearts be filled with the fullness of God. Amen.*

EMPOWERMENT

READING ACTS 1:1–14.
'"But you shall receive power when the Holy Spirit has come upon you . . ."' (v.8, NKJV).

YESTERDAY (*WOL* 22 APR) when dealing with the Great Commission, we began to touch on this concept of empowerment. When we receive a personal commission from someone we admire, love, and respect, the motivation to fulfil that commission is much greater than merely doing something just because it is right. It also more readily produces joy and fulfilment.

Yet there is more to empowerment than a personal call from someone respected and loved. Specific directions are needed about what to do. Jesus told his followers they were to 'make disciples' (Matt. 28:19); 'make disciples' is the verb and it is in the aorist imperative tense, which means that this is not a matter for discussion. Disciples are commanded by Christ to go and make disciples. They are to make disciples by going out to the people, baptising them in the name of the triune God. Mark tells us that the disciple is to teach by preaching the gospel (Mark 16:15); Luke adds that the gospel is essentially the preaching of the life, suffering, and resurrection of Christ (cf Luke 24:46,47). In John's account of the restoration of Peter, we learn that in fulfilling the Great Commission the disciples are to be like shepherds caring for their sheep (John 21:17), not like masters ruling over their subjects.

Empowerment comes from a personal commission combined with specific instructions. But there is still more to divine empowerment, disciples are to be anointed by the Holy Spirit himself (v.8); that is filled with all the fullness of God. This is the ultimate expression of discipleship in terms of a personal relationship with Christ. Through the Spirit, he never leaves us but is with us to the end of the age. Through the indwelling of the Spirit, we have power to preach the gospel.

PRAYER *Lord, grant us the desire to be your disciples, and grant us the power to fulfil your great commission.*
Let the light of the gospel shine through us. Amen.

PRAYER SUBJECT *Family members and friends who need Christ.*

THE AUTHORITY OF EXPERIENCE(1)

READING ACTS 22:12–16
'You will be his witness to all men of what you have seen and heard' (v.15, NIV).

cf John 4:29,39   PROCLAIMING THE GOSPEL was never intended to be a matter of debate and argument, even though these methods have their places. Supremely, the gospel has been communicated by the word of a witness speaking as sincerely and truthfully as possible of the things he or she has seen and heard.

17:1ff   Although Paul was a master in debate, as his brief stay in Athens revealed, he obviously felt the weakness of that approach because when he arrived in Corinth from Athens, he resolved only to talk about the crucified

1 Cor 2:1–5   Christ. Experience, providing it has the correct checks and balances, possesses a tremendous authority in communicating the gospel. As Paul spoke with the hostile crowd in Jerusalem they listened intently, even allowing him to refer to Jesus as the 'Righteous One',

v.14   that is the Messiah, they could not gainsay his personal witness. It was only when he spoke of his mission to the

v.21   Gentiles that their anger erupted again.

One of the great advantages of this God-given procedure of witnessing to what we have seen and heard, (both words carry the meanings of experience), is that

cf Mark 5:19,20   the exercise is one which can engage everyone. Quite correctly we regard the promise of the Holy Spirit's empowering as being for all of God's people; it follows therefore, that the command to witness is also for us all.

1:8; *Wol* 23 Apr   We can all share with someone or other, that which we have experienced of our Lord.

TO PONDER   *Blessèd Lord, to see thee truly,*
Then to tell as I have seen,
This shall rule my life supremely,
This shall be the sacred gleam.
(Albert Orsborn, SASB 591)

AUTHORITY OF EXPERIENCE (2)

READING ACTS 22:12–16
'You will be his witness to all men of what you have seen and heard' (v.15, NIV).

AN UNDUE EMPHASIS on experience, particularly personal experience can be dangerous. History records the damage done to the faith and groups of people who have fallen under the spell of some charismatic leader for whom experience, his own, of course, has been the supreme arbiter of truth and morality. The message given to Paul by Ananias contained its own special safeguard, 'to all men of what you have seen and heard.'

Implicit in this statement is the experience of the current community of God's people. If Paul was to belong to the whole people of God he could not separate himself from them, and neither did he. In the earlier account of his conversion it seems obvious that he benefited in fellowship and counsel from other followers of Jesus. Although Paul was to receive revelations through the Holy Spirit of enormous significance to the entire Church, and, in his desire to make it clear that he had had a direct revelation from Jesus, he stated he consulted no man, the crucial fact remains that his experience, so visionary, practical and spiritual, was in harmony with the experience of his peers.

9:19–30

v.14
Gal 1:16

An added strand in Paul's experience and a prime safeguard is that it was consistent with Old Testament teaching, and the teaching of our Lord. The more we know of Paul, the more we know of Jesus and the Old Testament. Experience of this nature carries immense authority because the Spirit of God is in it.

We are not divided,
All one body we,
One in hope, in doctrine,
One in charity.
(Sabine Baring-Gould, SASB 690)

TO PONDER

THE WONDER OF EXPERIENCE

READING ACTS 22:12–16
"Then he said, 'The God of our fathers has chosen you to know his will and to see the Righteous One and to hear words from his mouth'" (v.14, NIV).

Ps 19:1

IT IS INCREDIBLE that God should allow us the opportunity to know him. We can look at creation and make deductions about him but through the centuries many have looked there and made inaccurate deductions. However, God, through his love and mercy has made it possible for ordinary people like us, as well as extraordinary people like Paul, to know him and acquire a rich experience of him.

Jer 29:13

God grants us this privilege in response to our search for him. If we seek him with all our hearts he will be found of us. His word assures us of the divine presence, and, being with him, we share communion.

Isa 43:2; Matt
28:20

> *O that I might know thee,*
> *Know thee as thou art;*
> *Know the love that owns me,*
> *Binds me to thy heart.*

God answers that heartfelt prayer. As we stay in communion with him, we discover new and deeper depths in his nature; a new and greater capacity within ourselves for love, change and achievement; a larger understanding of our role in the extension of his Kingdom. We learn to prove God in the ordinary circumstances of life, and from that proven base of the relevance and sufficiency of God, we move out with confidence to witness to others about him.

PRAYER

> *O that I might show thee,*
> *Show thy love to all,*
> *Show the love that owns me;*
> *Consummates my call.*

THE STRATEGY

READING ACTS 22:19–22
'Then the Lord said to me, "Go; I will send you far away to the Gentiles"'
(v.21, NIV).

FROM THE BEGINNING God had a strategy to fulfil: the
Gentiles also were to receive the divine love and grace.
Happily, the Old Testament was not silent on this crucial
development. From the call of Abraham, 'all peoples on
earth will be blessed through you'; to the prophets, 'I will   Gen 12:3b
also make you a light for the Gentiles, that you may bring
my salvation to the ends of the earth'; the emphases within   Isa 49:6; cf
the ministry of Jesus, 'God so loved the world . . .'; through   Hos 2:23
the Acts of the Apostles which saw the commencement   John 3:16
and consolidation of this strategy, we perceive the hand of   11:1–18
God, who is the creator and Father of all mankind.

Paul was marvellously well-equipped for the task
given him by the risen Lord. Fluent in Greek because
of his upbringing in a large commercial city; nurtured in
the Jewish faith, first in Tarsus and then Jerusalem;
converted to Christianity in a Gentile city; possessed of
enormous courage and initiative, and, seemingly, a born
traveller. His job description as the Apostle to the
Gentiles fitted him admirably.

We who are Gentiles have cause to be grateful to Paul.
Largely through him, the faith crossed the first continen-
tal barrier, and, since then, he has been a source of   16:6–12
inspiration to all who have helped make Christianity into
a worldwide faith. And is he not an example to us as we
accept our calling to witness for Christ wherever he
wants us to be?

> To thee I all my powers present,   AFFIRMATION
> That for thy truth they may be spent;
> Fulfil thy sovereign counsel, Lord;
> Thy will be done, thy name adored.
>   (Johann Joseph Winckler,
>   trs John Wesley, SASB 526)

INTERROGATION BY WHIP

READING ACTS 22:22–9

'The commander ordered Paul to be taken into the barracks. He directed that he be flogged and questioned in order to find out why the people were shouting at him like this' (v.24, NIV).

THE COURAGEOUS PAUL was entitled to be more than a little concerned when he heard this command. It was common practice by the Romans to use a special whip, its lashes laced with pieces of stone and bone, in order to extract the truth from a prisoner. This fearsome flogging frequently led to the death of the victim, or, if not death, the victim was maimed for life. Clearly, it was time for Paul to make his Roman citizenship count: even as they stretched him on the frame to flog him, he asked the question which released him from that brutality.

v.25

The punishment Paul was about to receive was all part of the price and privilege of being a witness. Had the commander 'examined' (the word has judicial overtones) Paul by this flogging, Paul would have used this harrowing experience further to implement his role as a witness. The Greek word which is translated 'witness' is the same word from which we receive our English word 'martyr'. Paul narrowly escaped fulfilling both meanings of the word on this occasion.

v.24, AV, RSV, NASB, REB

All too soon, Paul, the faithful witness, was to become Paul the faithful martyr but before then he had much to do for his Lord. There was to be his witness in Jerusalem, on the road to Rome, and in Rome itself, and he still had to write some of his greatest letters. Paul's time had not yet come.

AFFIRMATION

Give me thy strength, O God of power,
Then winds may blow, or thunders roar,
Thy faithful witness will I be;
'Tis fixed, I can do all through thee.

(Johann Joseph Winckler,
trs John Wesley, SASB 526)

SATURDAY 29 APRIL
INVERTED VALUES

READING ACTS 22:22–9
'As they stretched him out to flog him, Paul said to the centurion standing there, "Is it legal for you to flog a Roman citizen who hasn't even been found guilty"' (v.25, NIV).

PAUL'S QUESTION highlights an unpleasant insight concerning the judicial system of that day. A non-Roman could die under this cross-examination by flogging, at the word or even whim of a relatively junior officer in the army. Our modern method of giving prisoners rights   v.24 has much to commend it. To be examined by flogging simply meant that the punishment would cease from the moment the interrogators felt that the victim had told the   v.29 truth. Presumably, if they remained unconvinced, they would continue with the flogging until the prisoner either died, or gave the answers they wanted to hear.

Wisely, Paul revealed his Roman citizenship, using its special privileges to protect himself. To the Romans, it mattered nothing that Paul was representative of the living God, but it mattered everything that he was a Roman citizen. It represents an inverted scale of values common to every age.

The commander obviously bought his citizenship for a large sum of money. Although his way to citizenship gave him equal rights with any other Roman, to be born a citizen, as was Paul, would carry a little more kudos. Paul's intended flogging never took place because the   v.28 commander knew he was accountable to the authorities for the treatment of a Roman citizen, but was unaware of the fact that he was accountable to God for his treatment of an ambassador of the King of Kings.

The Lord of life was crucified,   TO PONDER
It was expedient he should die, (John 18:14, NASV)
And from his cross suspended high,
Beheld his wounds and he was satisfied, (Isa 53:11)
Rose from his tomb and gave us Eastertide!

WORDS OF PRAYER

READING PSALM 130:1–8
'I wait for the Lord, my soul waits, and in his word I put my hope' (v.5, NIV).

AS THE PILGRIM PEOPLE made their way to Jerusalem for one or
other of the great feasts they sang the Psalms headed by the words, 'A
song of ascents'. When they commenced their pilgrimage they were
quite possibly in the right frame of mind, but by the time they arrived,
with the singing and conversation on the day, they would be totally
prepared for the festival. This Psalm, however, represents an ascent
out of the abyss of despair (v.1). The Psalmist was conscious of his
sins (v.3); had made his cry for mercy; and, seemingly, God had not
responded. He was therefore waiting for God; waiting with hope, but
nevertheless becoming increasingly anxious (vv.5,6). The Psalmist's
experience links him with every generation.

> *Wait for the Lord, my soul, in quietness,*
> *Hold firm thy restlessness with reins of peace.*
> *He is the God of wholeness, not of stress,*
> *With him is harmony: all discords cease.*
> *Await his coming in full confidence*
> *That when he comes, his timing will be right,*
> *He tarries not because of diffidence*
> *But only that you live by faith, not sight.*
>
> *My soul, this waiting time is for your good,*
> *You need to use the grace already given,*
> *You must grow strong, as all God's children should,*
> *If you would walk with him from earth to heaven.*
>
> *Wait thou, and in thy waiting be content,*
> *For he will come, the Lord omnipotent.*

PRAYER *My heart tells me, O Lord, that you are never distant*
from me; simply that there are times when I am unaware
of you. Help me to hold on in faith and not be too
dependent upon my feelings, and help me to cultivate a
sense of your presence. In Jesus' name. Amen.

PRAYER SUBJECT *Those engaged in prison chaplaincies.*

INDEX
(as from January 1992)

NOTE: Selected Scripture passages are used for the extended coverage given to each of the great Christian festivals from which each separate volume takes its name. Sundays and the New Year are also given separate treatment, too varied to be included in a general index.